BE THE GATEWAY
A Practical Guide to Sharing Your Creative Work and Engaging an Audience

By Dan Blank

Table of Contents

Introduction

When I talk to a creative professional for the first time, I often hear the same concern: they are overwhelmed and feel stuck. They dream of their potential, and how their creative work can help and entertain others. The problem lies in how they measure their success. They seek validation from big institutions, bestseller lists, sales numbers, and high-profile media. They measure how the world accepts them with followers, re-shares, reviews, likes, and favorites.

They measure by numbers.

I want to reframe how you think about creating and sharing your work, and I want you to disregard numbers. When you lie on your deathbed and someone asks about the work you are most proud of, I don't want you to think of a bestseller list. I want you to think about specific experiences that indicate that you and your work connected with, and influenced, the lives of others.

I want you to remember names and faces, and moments with these people, not how many followers you had on a social network. I want you to remember that you were a gateway for others which led them to places that shaped who they are, and made their lives better.

Let's begin the journey …

Section 1: You Are a Gateway

Creative Work is a Journey

How do you measure the success of your creative work? Often when we think of what we hope to achieve, we look for shorthand to represent this:

- It may be an **object** that represents the culmination of your effort in a physical form. If you are a writer, this could be holding a book that you wrote in your hands; if you sell crafts, it could be seeing your business logo enlarged on a twenty-foot sign as you prepare for a huge craft show.
- It may be a **token** of success, such as an award you win or a plaque that represents a milestone you reached.
- It may be a **metric**, such as reaching the top of a best seller list, surpassing a certain amount of sales for your work, or a certain "follower" count on a social network.

While these things represent what you hope for your work, they shouldn't be the goal. They are public milestones the world can see and appreciate, but they mask the true impact of your work. These milestones help validate who we are, and in the process, we hope that reaching them will unlock a "next level" of success—a level where it becomes easier to create our work, to share it, and to engage others.

We calculate that objects, tokens, and metrics will ensure that greater success will now come with less effort, but that doesn't happen.

Most people are paralyzed by questions about goals, such as, "Where do you want to be in five years?" It's a scary question, because it represents not just what we want to accomplish, but who we want to become. So we default to defining our goals via objects, tokens, and metrics. If I ask a writer about their goals, it is easier to just say the phrase "I want to be published," "I want to win an award," or "I want to be a bestseller." They can envision the book on their desk, an award on their shelf, or a page torn out of a newspaper where their name appears on the top of a bestseller list.

The artist may say, "I want a gallery show," and a musician's dream may be to hear their songs on the radio. These are common markers for "success," and are simplified versions of a reality the creator hopes to experience. But these markers are often hollow; they don't lead to the feeling of validation or success that these artists hoped for. Rather, they create a sense of impostor syndrome — that their achievement was a fluke, and that soon the world will realize they didn't deserve the accolades. Instead of feeling validated, someone with impostor syndrome is riddled with anxiety that they will be revealed as a fraud, and that they can never live up to the success people now expect of them.

This is what I have found after speaking to thousands of creative professionals over the years. A writer may have had their books published by large houses, received stellar reviews, been featured in national media, and won awards, yet their work didn't sell well. Their lives before and after the book, remained unchanged. They may not only feel they are "back at square one," but feel they are digging out of a hole, worse off than when they started, because of the stigma of failure. Even those authors who did find success with sales can still seem confused as to why the book worked, who their audience is, and how to follow it up. They feel naked and exposed, worried that they will "mess up" a success that they barely understand.

The same applies to a musician whose song is played on the radio, but who can't fill a mid-sized venue for a concert; the artist who gets a gallery show, but whose work fails to sell; or the crafter featured on a prominent website, but who struggles to make sales and develop a following.

Achieving these traditional markers for success — objects, tokens, and metrics — can make someone feel *more* lost, because they assumed this process would unlock something new for them, and instead, nothing is different. They hoped that validation would spark a profound sense of self-esteem, yet they may feel less sure of themselves than ever. They may have assumed that selling their next idea would be easier, and it isn't; that access to media and publicity is easier, and it isn't; that they would earn more money with less effort, and they can't.

To solve this, people often focus on marketing and social media. They have heard stories of the person whose status update or photo has "gone viral," and decide that they want to go viral as well. They want to wake up one day and find that thousands of people have discovered their work magically, overnight. At the very least, they begin to look at every social media update as a press release that could hit the right person at the right time. However, this can create an additional pressure. Creative professionals often feel confusion over developing a "platform" around their work. They don't know what to include on a website, what to send in an email newsletter, what to share on social media, and how to make marketing feel meaningful.

Even further, they feel their pure creative vision has been corrupted by this "requirement" to market their work. They are told left and right that a publisher won't buy their book unless they have 10,000 Twitter followers. Artists feel they are somehow "less than" because someone else breaks out on Etsy, while they can barely sell six prints of their art, all six to family and friends. Their biggest shock is that it was hard work even to get those six people to buy it.

I want to offer you the solution I share with creative professionals I work with every day. It's a simple phrase:

Be the gateway.

Instead of framing the value of your work by how it performs in the market, you define it by how other people experience the world through your creative work — the stories and experiences you share, and the topics you talk about. This simple idea radically shifts the value of what you create. Instead of selling a product in a marketplace, you become the gateway for how your work can shape the world for others, and inspire them.

Regardless of your creative medium, you are a storyteller, right? Then use that gift. I don't mean that just for oral or written storytellers — artists, musicians, crafters, filmmakers, and photographers all tell stories with their work.

Reframe success so it isn't about seeking validation from massive audiences, but rather how you reach one person. The people I see who succeed focus on one-on-one engagement with other people, not on going viral. To be a gateway is to find success by focusing on the human side of that which engages people, what it means to have your work truly shape the lives of others, and what it means to feel fulfilled as a creator.

The concept applies to all types of creative work. The novelist who comes to embody a message such as the underdog always triumphs. The memoir author who finds humor in tragedy, and doesn't just tell her story, but helps others navigate their own. The nonfiction author whose work reshapes how someone thinks, and therefore, lives. The artist whose philosophy doesn't just serve as the foundation for painting, but for seeing the world in a new way. The musician who inspires with a song, but also champions causes that her fans believe in. A filmmaker whose process of craft becomes a blueprint for how his fans can approach their own creative vision. Regardless of the medium or craft, the effect of these people goes beyond the work itself—they somehow help others make sense out of life.

When you frame your focus as a gateway instead of an object, token, or metric, it helps you identify what you want to do. You get to focus on an experience to create, not just a milestone you dream of. The difference? You can take action to connect with people who love your work via your gateway *right now*. You can take clear actions day by day, week by week, to reach the people who care about your work. When you create as a gateway, success immediately becomes more accessible.

Being a gateway is a higher calling than an object, token, or metric. It's also more fun.

Your work can open up possibilities for others and forge new paths that had never before been considered. Don't just throw "products" out into the marketplace; change the way people see the world through your creative work.

Think of it this way: a book is really a conversation that happens in the reader's head. It is half what the author intended, and half how the reader translates it. No two people read the same book the same way. We come with biases, with needs, with a unique lifetime of experiences. The same holds true for a song. The songwriter may craft lyrics thinking of a breakup they went through, but the person listening to it can only think of their *own* relationships. The song is an interplay between the intention of the artist and the experience and context of the person listening to it.

When I meet creative professionals who want help in

reaching their audience, I don't ask about their goals, but instead say, "Tell me about the conversations you would *love* to be having with others." If I asked about their goals, they would feel forced to talk about achievements for themselves alone. Instead, I want to focus on how their creative work can have a powerful effect on others. How it can truly change the lives of thousands of people.

Sometimes we assume that an achievement represents this — it doesn't. Bestseller lists can be gamed; too often creative work is purchased, but never noticed (books are purchased and not read, art is purchased, but never hung, etc.). Your work can win an award, and fail to find an audience. You can get an incredible review and have it lead to zero new fans. You can be on national TV and have it lead to only a handful of new sales.

Being a gateway is about ensuring your work truly connects with others in the most meaningful way possible, instead of being treated as nothing more than a product swiped across the bar code scanner at the food store.

Are you ready? Let's dig in…

Experience Creates a Story

Many people have stood in front of a mirror, hairbrush in hand, pretending they were a famous singer on stage. If you haven't, you've likely daydreamed about a big achievement. You have envisioned the moment when you went from zero to hero.

I don't care about that moment.

Sure, I have heard all the motivational stories of people who visualized their success, and had it come true. In the years before cartoonist Scott Adams became successful with his comic *Dilbert*, he would look himself in the mirror, repeating affirmations—simple sentences such as "I, Scott Adams will become a syndicated cartoonist." The idea is that simply by repeating it, he made the achievement more likely to happen.[1]

Actor Jim Carrey would visualize his success when he was still a struggling actor. One time he even wrote a check out to himself for $10 million dollars "for acting services rendered." He kept it in his wallet, and within five years, he was earning more than that.[2]

Those stories are inspiring, to be sure, but between those two things—visualizing their dream and achieving it—was a journey. One filled with hard work, talent, important connections, and some luck. Frodo didn't just magically end up on Mount Doom to dispose of the ring, and Harry Potter didn't just wake up one day a wizard in control of his powers. Each had to take a journey to test themselves, to learn, and to develop clarity in their focus. They also needed help from others. That is where they connected their dream to reality.

This is the moment I care about.

What is *your* story? Share the process and your journey as it happens.

But before you run out and start a blog where you detail every struggle you have with your work, you need to pause and identify how your story relates to the gateway you're crafting. This is not just about over-sharing your days on social media. It is not about revealing every moment you experience self-doubt. It is about understanding the connection between what you create, why you create it, and how it will engage others. This is the "secret" to engaging others, which is not really a secret at all. It is as old as human culture and how we are wired.

What you are doing is building a path to your gateway. One that is wide enough, well-lit enough, and signals to people that it is worth continuing down because right around the corner is what they seek ... your gateway. The marker that will lead them to what they are searching for.

For instance, as I write this book, I am sharing photos of myself writing and editing on Instagram and Twitter, explaining that I am writing the book. Each day, people see what my process for writing looks like: it is about showing up each day to do the work. It is about building a habit that is practical and accessible. People who follow along not only come to understand that I am writing a book and what it is about, but they begin to feel as they are a part of the process. For my audience — creative professionals — it illustrates the process. It brings them behind the scenes, and creates a story around it. That story is not, "Ugh, here is yet another author promoting their book to me." It is more like, "Here is Dan at Starbucks each morning at 5:30, slowly crafting his book." In other words, instead of feeling promoted to, they may resonate with the slow process to create meaningful work. For me, the creator, I have people who are following along with the journey, even as I write the book.

That is a powerful connection for someone to have with your work. Consider how if you watch one of those singing or talent shows on TV, and one of the contestants is from your home town, that simple connection makes you root for them. Why? Partly because of hometown pride, but also because it may mean that if this person can reach for enormous success, you can, too. When you share your journey, you are building advocates in the process; those who aren't just aware of what you are doing, but feel connected to it in a personal way. When it comes time for you to release your creative work, you will have a crowd of people ready to help it spread.

Many creative professionals take the opposite approach. They hide away in complete silence for months or years and then make a big announcement: "I landed an agent," "I signed with a publisher," or "My book is being released tomorrow." They are banking on the impact of a single announcement instead of sharing an authentic look at how their creative vision aligns with what their ideal audience dreams about. One of these versions tells a better *story* than the other, and it also slowly develops an audience for your work.

Later in the book, we will dig into exactly how to do this, and how to avoid common pitfalls. There is a difference between clearly communicating and developing advocates, and over-sharing every thought you have and meal you eat.

I would encourage you to focus on sharing experiences you have, because this is indeed how stories are created. Focus on conversations you have, because this is where you are already connecting to others on that authentic human level. Focus on how you can connect with others today around your work. How you are curious, how you are developing your skills, how you are relishing moments where you feel inspired.

Focus on adding value to the lives of others, of sharing the experience your work is meant to create for them.

Sharing what you do in an engaging manner is different than so much of the advice that overwhelms creative professionals: build a brand, launch a newsletter, use hashtags, game your sales ranking, etc.

Instead of dreaming up some "big brand" you want to create, simply document and share what you are passionate about. This encourages you to be aware of how your daily life aligns to your creative work. It forces you to be accountable for attending to it. When you share what drives you and how you attend to your creative work, it prevents you from getting lost in the dream. What I mean by this is, those people who spend all of their time dreaming about the creative work they hope to create, but never find the time to actually do it. This could be a writer who constantly updates social media with writing tips and motivational quotes, but barely finds time to write themselves. The musician who seeks success, but hasn't practiced or recorded anything in months. The person who keeps developing an idea for their craft business, but is doing only business planning, and no actual crafting and no interaction with people they hope to reach.

I can't tell you how many people I have seen who will try to "build their brand" on something, and when you scratch the surface, you find that they are advocates for something they don't do themselves. Why? Because they found it easier to advocate for something than they did to actually do it. They jumped in front of a parade, but have not done the work to lead it anywhere or connect with anyone.

This classic writing advice applies to how you share your work: "Show, don't tell." Meaning, don't sell me on your work by telling me how great it is; instead, show me the process, show me why your work matters to you, and how it can connect to what I care about.

Actor John Malkovich characterized this as a distinction between ambition and drive:

> *"I think of ambition as the need to prove something to others, and the need to be recognized. A need for rewards outside of the work. Drive motivates you to do whatever it is you're doing as well as you can."*[3]

So many creative works—novels, movies, songs—open us up to new worlds, characters, and stories that help us experience our own lives in new ways, and help us develop our own sense of self. How often have you thought of a character from a book or movie as inspiration in your life? Think about it this way: why do people get tattoos of a favorite literary quote, or a scene from a children's book? These symbols—these stories—align to narratives that the reader has about their own experience of life. As a creative professional, you become the gateway for them to experience it.

This is why fans scream and cry when J.K. Rowling walks into a room. She is a gateway for a worldview that has shaped people's lives. The characters she has crafted embody who we hope to be, or someone we deeply relate to. The stories delve into deeper issues in ways that feel inspirational and accessible.

A few years back, I met J.K. Rowling at one of her rare public appearances. When I first heard of the event—a conversation between her and Ann Patchett in the gorgeous Alice Tully Hall in New York City's Lincoln Center—I stalked the phone lines and website for when tickets would become available, and when they did, I managed to get seven tickets. After I secured the tickets, I saw that their value in the aftermarket skyrocketed. I could easily pocket hundreds of dollars in profit, and still get to see J.K. Rowling for free, because of the profits I made selling the other tickets.

But I couldn't. That wasn't the type of thing you do for a J.K. Rowling event; that isn't the type of thing you do to other J.K. Rowling fans. Instead, I considered what would be the *right* thing to do in this instance. Because honestly, when tickets went on sale, I grabbed as many tickets as I could, in a mad panic. I had no plan for them; excitement got the better of me.

I decided to give them away — well, all of them except for *my* ticket! I figured the best way to celebrate what J.K. Rowling had created was to bring joy to those who love her. I did that in three ways. First, I held a giveaway on my blog for two of the tickets, as a way to reward my readers. For the remaining four tickets, I decided to be more selective — I offered them to two friends who are enormous supporters of children's literature and writers. Then, I asked one of them who else I should offer them to, giving her the opportunity to surprise and delight two of her friends.

It's funny how much joy you can create when you focus first on the experience you can craft instead of the profit you can earn.

That night, we all met up in front of Lincoln Center and chatted about books. We lapped up every moment of the conversation between Ms. Rowling and Ann on stage. Then, we waited in line with hundreds of other people to meet Ms. Rowling and have a book signed.

This was where the magic happened.

It wasn't that Ms. Rowling did anything special. She greeted each fan, signed a book, made brief banter, and kept the line moving. The magic came from the fans. Many were dressed up, others had made gifts for her, and each had practiced what they would say to her when their moment arrived. There was one twenty-something guy who I watched all evening clutch the letter he wanted to give her. He had sealed it with a wax seal.

What was clear is that she has come to represent something to her fans. She has become a lightning rod for belief systems, for a worldview. She has become the gateway for how her fans experience the world, experience each other, and experience themselves.

Too often, I hear this line from a novelist: "Oh, I just want to entertain people!" This is an excuse they are giving that belittles the scope of what a story does for readers. Should it entertain? Sure. But that alone is not how we experience stories.

Stories help us make sense of the world. Characters embody aspects of who we hope to become. When we read about Harry Potter and his hidden gifts; when we read about Jason Bourne and his search for self and truth; when we read about experiencing true love in *The Notebook*, this is not just "entertainment." It is something so much more.

As a creative professional, consider what those things are. That what you share within your creative work — and outside of it — can embody the deeper themes that drive you, and that engage your ideal audience.

Let me give you a model for how to think about this. I framed it this way for a client of mine who is a memoir writer and trying to figure out how to shape their story and their platform. These are three elements that connect the work you are crafting to being a gateway for readers in the platform you develop.

1. **STORY.** The first goal is to be a storyteller — to craft a compelling story. Again, this is regardless of the medium you work in. This is obvious for the memoir example, since the book is laid out as a story. For a musician, it may be where a song takes the listener, or how an album explores a theme from ten different

directions. For an artist, it could be how a painting expresses an emotion, and how the gallery show, step by step, crafts a new way of seeing the world. For a photographer, perhaps a series is created that focuses on one group of people, one neighborhood, one narrative theme.

2. **CREATOR.** You become the gateway, the personal way through which the reader experiences a larger topic. You are the way in. This is not unique to memoir, but I think it applies here in a magnified way. For a musician, there is a reason that they are set up high on a stage, and all the seats in the room are facing them. Yes, the music is primary, but everyone focuses their eyes and attention on those playing the music. At a gallery show, there may be a crowd around the artist, where people ask questions about their work. While the work does stand alone, the artist helps to explain it in a way that allows someone to better appreciate it. The way a photographer captures an image adds to our appreciation of the image itself. I have seen many series of photographs on Instagram, or videos on YouTube, where a photographer shares their travel to a destination, the gear they use, and the nuance they used to capture and process an image. Again, this is a story that unfolds, not just an end result.

3. **TOPICS.** Then come the topics, the issues, the narratives that your story digs into. Memoirs can be about so many things, including overcoming huge challenges that others may experience, or that come to symbolize experiences the reader is going through. No, we weren't on that hiking trail with Cheryl Strayed, author of the memoir *Wild*, about her 1,000-mile solo trek on the Pacific Crest Trail. Nor did we join Elizabeth Gilbert, author of the memoir *Eat, Pray, Love* on

her journey to Italy, India, and Bali. But that doesn't stop these books from resonating deeply on a personal level with readers. For musicians, artists, and photographers, sometimes these topics or narrative themes are obvious, and other times they are buried. Figuring them out is part of how a fan engages with the work.

These three things work together to allow the "platform" to be the gateway for people. For instance, while writing this book, I became obsessed with the song "The Only Living Boy in New York," by Simon and Garfunkel. I heard it played it at Starbucks, and was reminded how much I liked the sound of the song, and the feeling of isolation and loneliness it provided. I thought of how incredible it was that both Paul Simon and Art Garfunkel were both still alive—I headed to Wikipedia to see how old they were and what they were up to. Then I added the song to a Spotify playlist. On the third or fourth listen in a week, I began to wonder what the song was really about, so I Googled the song's meaning. It turns out, Paul Simon wrote it as the duo were breaking up after nearly thirteen years together; Art Garfunkel was turning his attention to an acting career. The song speaks specifically to how Art was delayed on a movie shoot, and how Paul was waiting for him to return. It was the last song they recorded for their final album together. This had me considering how difficult transitions are, and how to navigate them gracefully in my own life.[4]

In listening to a single song, I experienced the STORY, the CREATORS, and the TOPIC that surround it. They are related ways of engaging with the song, each level deeper and more personal than the next.

This is what you should craft for your work.

Let's look at another example, turning back to memoir. If

you are writing a memoir about your experience with cancer, you don't have to write an email newsletter that steals its content from the book. Instead, you can tell other people's stories of their experiences with cancer. Or tell stories about overcoming the odds, or dig into the many other themes that are likely buried within your book. The platform you develop around a book should not try to re-create it—what you share online and in person should not just steal all of the stories you share in the book itself. Instead, it should tap into aspects of the story, and then extend them in new ways that the book could not.

This relates to social media as well. Too often, we use it to comment on news stories, and merely share links. Instead, use it to tell a story—an original story—that opens up a worldview for people.

If you are that memoir writer whose book is about cancer, and a key theme is medical reform, don't just link to articles in newspapers. Instead, find and tell stories that resonate with us. Become the voice for others ... the gateway for them to share their stories with the world. I mean, how powerful is that? To not be the 1,000th person to share the link to a newspaper article, but to be the first person to tell someone's story that needs to be heard?

Awhile back I worked with author Lauri Taylor to bring her memoir, *The Accidental Truth: What My Mother's Murder Investigation Taught Me About Life*, to the world. Lauri is amazing—she has this innate ability to connect with people. Again and again, she would tell me about a meeting she had with someone about her book, and she invariably described the highlight of the meeting as this:

"We cried."

Why? Because by sharing her story with that person, Lauri became a gateway for them to share their own experiences. While Lauri's memoir is unique to her specific experience, she hits a nerve with others who have lost a family member.

Do you need to go around, and find one person at a time to cry with in order to affect others with your book? No.

But look at the Amazon page for Lauri's book, which has more than 100 reviews, averaging out to 4.7 out of 5 stars. That is an incredibly high rating for a book on Amazon. The book touches people. Just as when you meet Lauri in person, you get a compelling sense of someone who is a gateway to a meaningful experience of our lives, including the crazy twists and turns that we all go through, Lauri validates that for readers, and when they meet her, they can't help but share their own stories.

Let's face it, this is why someone crafts creative work — they become a gateway for others. When people walk through the gateway, they enjoy powerful benefits:

- They experience a compelling story or experience
- They see the world in a new way
- They shape their own identity

That last one is huge. You are a gateway to the identity that someone wants for themselves, or that highlights an aspect of themselves they want to be more clear, more in the forefront, more real. Even if your work takes years to craft, you can still be a gateway right now. Even to one person. Or to dozens. Or hundreds. Or thousands. Opening up their world. Their identity. Their experience. Their connection to others.

Some of you may be thinking, "Dan, I want my work to speak for itself. I don't want to have to consider my audience, and engage with them, nor do I myself want to represent what they love in my work." I tend to think that this is a romantic view of how creative work is crafted, published, discovered, and consumed.

Sure, Bob Dylan's *Blood on the Tracks* is a perfect album, but it also came after thousands of live shows, interviews, collaborations, and deals with partners such as record labels. Is the music itself a gateway? Yes, of course. But so are thousands of other actions that Dylan takes in a given year to ensure that his music is heard.

Even when we find someone's narrative that seems more "pure" about the strength of the art itself finding an audience, a gateway is still present. J.K. Rowling wrote Harry Potter alone in a cafe, struggling to make ends meet. She submitted it to publishers without any form of what we would call "platform." Yet she is very active on Twitter, has forged movie deals, created an online community with Pottermore, has partnerships with all kinds of media, and even a theme park. It wasn't enough for her to just let the books reach readers; she has created complex gateways to ensure it finds new audiences, and that the audience who already love the books can experience the world they have created in new ways.

When someone experiences any creative work — a book, art, music, photography, etc. — it is an act of co-creation. The creator has crafted it with a vision in mind, but the person who experiences it does so through the filter of their own life. They interpret it in ways unique to themselves. If you and I each listen to the same song, we each may interpret it in different ways. We may experience different emotions at different points in the song, and we may feel differently about it based on our individual experience with music or the artist themselves.

For instance, if you walk into the studio of a master carpenter, they are telling you a story that is co-created. They aren't just showing you a product in a way that is purely objective. Your experience of the process shapes how you feel about it. Maybe you had to drive an hour to get to their workshop, and discover it is in a converted century-old barn.

That experience may shape how you feel about the cabinets you are about to see. Even without being fully conscious of it, you may feel that you are seeking a cabinet that is unique and made just for you, not a commodity that everyone else purchases at a big box retail store. The craftsperson may begin by telling you about the trees that their wood comes from, then show you the rough-hewn boards that they have stored for years. How they found those boards may be a story in itself; perhaps they were reclaimed wood from an 18th century house. Then they begin to illustrate the techniques they use to shape these boards. They show you a vintage sanding plane they use, and ask you to feel its weight. They tell you about the eighty-year-old man they purchased it from at an estate sale.

In each step of this process, they are co-creating a story around their work. Half happens in the work itself, half happens in your head. This is how you filter it through your own experience, personality, desires, and fears.

Two different people can visit that carpenter and walk away with different conclusions. One may feel they have tapped into something deeply needed in this world — and their kitchen — old-world craftsmanship that will last for a century. Another may feel that the carpenter is an overpriced charlatan, because anyone can nail together a few boards of wood.

Through your creative work, you get to craft the stories of how others find and engage with it. Your art, your craft is not objective — it will be experienced by different people in different ways. You get to shape that, and it becomes the gateway for others. Now, let's consider how these stories align to the identities that your audience seeks.

Stories Create the Identity Your Audience Seeks

Too often, we think our intended audience wants value alone. We imagine that they are constantly looking out for a "great deal," and if we offer them something more useful at a cheaper price, that is the secret to success. But for those working in the creative arts, that isn't the case. What does your audience want, more than anything? An identity.

They want to feel cool.
They want to feel creative.
They want to feel free.
They want to feel as though they live by a deep moral code.
They want to feel they are the real deal.
They want to be old school.
They want to be cutting edge.
They want to be compassionate.
They want to be unwavering.
To have an identity is to feel special — to feel alive — to feel whole — to feel worthwhile — to feel potential.

People don't buy things; they buy the *feeling* that things give them. They are investing in the building blocks of their own identity, and how this helps creates narratives they can show others. Perhaps they buy the same model guitar as Slash uses, because it evokes a narrative of them being "the real deal" like he is, even though you can perform the same song on any of thousands of different guitars. Or perhaps they use Emeril's recipe and ingredients because it allows them to tell the narrative that they are as caring and skillful as he is, even though there are hundreds of recipes for the same dish.

Your audience lives by narratives. This is how they express their identity. They want a narrative that makes sense of the world. It is not just a reflection on the world, but their place within it. It justifies their decisions. It allays their fears. It motivates their hopes.

Being a fan of Batman provides the identity of living by a code, of being brave, of having a hidden side that is noble. Too often a creator will try to sell this fan a great deal, or a clever idea, but what the fan really wants is to find a way to align to their narrative and identity more clearly. This is why people get Batman tattoos. Why they wear a simple shirt with the Batman insignia. Why they argue over which version of Batman is the one definitive version, or why Batman is better than Superman.

Once, I walked into the home of a friend, and there was a large display of Star Wars action figures on top of the shelving unit in their living room — a prominent place in their home. I asked about them, and I was told that when he was a kid, he was playing with firecrackers in his garage. He exploded a home-made "bomb" of LEGO pieces, which shot into his father's beloved car, dinging the paint. His dad, in a fit of rage, threw out his son's own most beloved possessions, dumping his Star Wars figures in the trash.

Here I was, twenty years later, in that son's home, where he has decided he can finally afford to collect them again. This wasn't about him buying possessions — it was about recapturing a narrative. One where he was a kid who could dream of being a hero, living in a universe where anything was possible. It was about finding simple joys. It aligns to his identity of adventure, of valor, of danger, or who he dreamed of being when he was eight.

I myself have collected toys my entire adult life, with LEGO being the only constant focus. The community of adults who collect LEGO have this phrase for the moment when someone begins playing with LEGO as an adult: they call it "coming out of the dark ages." The "dark ages" in this scenario are the years where you felt you couldn't play with LEGO because that was just for kids. Shame and embarrassment kept you from doing what you wanted.

Those adults who do come out of the dark ages aren't just buying a commodity, which is what LEGO tends to look like: thousands of primary colored objects, all in the same shape. Instead, they are aligning to narratives that they embrace. Narratives of creating anything you want, of crafting a smaller world that you can control when your adult world is anything but controllable.

Narratives define our reality. Perhaps the best example of this is sports. I respect the many wonderful things that sports create, such as the experience of teamwork, the value of practice, and so much else. But I have never actively followed any team or sport. This makes me feel like something of an anthropologist embedded in a strange culture. Sitting in a cafe, I will see an out-of-shape fifty-something talk about a professional team in terms of "we."

"We are going to kill you this Sunday."
"We had a good season."
"We got robbed."

The reality is that these fans did little to actually affect the game itself. They feel that their $40 sweatshirt somehow illustrates meaningful support. It doesn't. What they bought with that is an identity, a narrative that somehow the Yankees are different than the Red Sox. But they aren't. The rosters of these teams change each season, and it's only happenstance who plays on which team in a given year. Oddly, this is the most controversial thing I will say in this entire book.

Each team is a huge business that constantly buys and sells players and support staff to travel to different stadiums and play a game with the same rules. This isn't a group of guys from the Bronx battling a group of guys from Southie, where there is a real regional culture and pride. I remember how Johnny Damon seemed to make such a big deal about never going to the Yankees from the Red Sox. Yet a few short years later, that is exactly what he did, play for the Yankees. So did some of the most celebrated players in Red Sox history: Wade Boggs, Roger Clemens, and even Babe Ruth himself.

I will get feedback on this book about how wrong I am about the distinction between the Red Sox and Yankees fans. People will tell me how the Yankees just buy their way to success with deeper pockets. Or how the Red Sox fans are all talk and no talent. Yet it's the same contracted players playing the same game; they just happen to wear different colors. The narrative overshadows this. A die-hard Red Sox fan can't imagine a world where someone likes the Yankees, and vice versa.

In other words, the narrative a fan has in their head overshadows any objective observations about the teams, the league, or the game itself. This mentality is a stand-in. An easy way to feel pride, identity, and the thrill of the win or loss. It is an escape from the everyday responsibilities that they feel so little control over. It is a way to have an easy black-and-white challenge, whereas relationships in their everyday life — which are very gray — stump them. It is a way to feel uncompromising when their lives are filled with so much compromise. It is a way to always have a hopeful dream of victory because every game, every season is a clean slate. It is where the players are always young and in shape, where the leaders are constantly swapped in and out. Only the name of the team remains the same. You have a "New York" team comprised of players and a management staff from all over the world. You have a player who was on the arch rival's team the previous season, traded onto yours. You go from hating this person more than anyone, to becoming their biggest advocate.

We live our lives by a narrative. Everything is filtered through it. One person drives to Starbucks and sees it as their little escape, a sign that they have "made it" because they can buy their personalized drink for $4.50 each day. In a day that is otherwise controlled by others — their boss, their colleagues, their kids, their spouse — this Starbucks coffee is their moment of freedom.

Others drive by Starbucks and see it as pretentious, overpriced yuppie garbage, which they reject. In doing so, they uphold the belief that they are good, down-to-earth people, who won't pay more than a dollar for a cup of coffee because that means they aren't getting ripped off. When they drive past Starbucks to get their $1 cup of coffee at Quik Check, it is a statement about who they are, and about values they believe in.

The reality? It's just a cup of coffee. But how we perceive it changes everything.

When you consider how you are a gateway for others, understanding your narrative, understanding theirs, and connecting the two is inherently what you are offering.

Most creative professionals I speak with are nervous about the idea of developing an audience, because they assume it means they will have to become a salesperson who is always "pitching" an offer to people. But that isn't the goal for them, and it won't be for you. Instead, you will be offering people a chance to align with the narratives that engage them. When someone follows Elizabeth Gilbert on social media, they are doing so to experience an aspect of who they are; they are embracing a narrative that they believe in. I just checked her Facebook page and one of her recent posts breaks all normal status update conventions — it is more than 3,000 words long and ends with "I love you; let's do this." It is personal and honest, and to many people, that breaks through a sense of jaded overwhelm that they may feel about everyone else's Facebook posts. They may say to themselves, "Liz didn't just share a pithy update, she went deep and wouldn't edit herself. She says what she means and isn't afraid to 'go there,' even if it takes 3,000 words to do so. And you know what? She is the only person today who told me she loved me. I think people need to be kinder to each other, and that is exactly what she does."

When someone else shuns Elizabeth's message, it is because they feel she embodies a narrative they don't like. Maybe they read that same status update and think it is indulgent, or that when a stranger says they love you, that it is disingenuous. It's the exact same status update, but two different people will react to it based on their own internal narratives, passions, and fears.

Regardless, the "result" for her on Facebook to that specific status update was that 10,000 people clicked the "Like" button, 1,300 people commented on the post, and more than 4,000 people shared it on their own Facebook profiles.

How does all of this relate to your creative work — the book, art, craft, song, idea, or business you are creating? It is perhaps the foundation of what it means to be a gateway. You are not creating a "fan," or a customer. You are providing someone something much deeper, which is a sense of themselves and the world around them.

When you understand the narratives your ideal audience seeks, you know how to engage those people. You know how to grab their attention, you know how to get them to lean in, and to become so enamored that they can't help but tell their friends. And isn't that the heart of what creative professionals want? To not just get attention, but change people's lives and get people talking? It's more than just "word-of-mouth marketing," it is the idea that you are truly creating conversations around what you create.

This doesn't happen when you sell based on value or price. It happens when you provide a narrative, and therefore, an identity, that your audience seeks. How can you help them come out of their "dark ages?"

Find and Align Your Narratives

Your gateway is a signal to others. This is a guiding focus to provide clarity, not just to others, but to yourself. Let's craft the language and intention of your gateway. Again, I will use the example of an author, but this applies to all other creative professionals.

Identifying your narratives can feel like an impossibly difficult task. It requires a sense of self-awareness that people sometimes avoid. It can feel uncomfortable to analyze yourself. It forces you to confront the fact that the way you see the world is through a filter that makes sense to you personally, but is not the way the world actually is for everyone. For instance, an experienced artist who has sold her work successfully for three years may look at the marketplace and feel it is full of possibilities, since it is validating and celebrating her work. But an artist whose work fails to find an audience or buyers may look at the exact same marketplace and feel it is stagnant and unwelcoming. Each wakes up with a different narrative in their mind, without realizing that their personal experience is what shapes it.

Understanding and communicating your narratives is the next step in crafting your gateway. To find and align your narratives, I encourage you to identify what matters most to you across your entire life, not just in your creative work. You have only so many resources of time, energy and money. Too many people fail in their creative work because they don't accept and embrace that. Most people are overwhelmed with responsibilities, including family, career, health, community, home, and so much else. This is in addition to their creative work. When you consider the narratives which drive you, it can't be just for your creative work, it has to be for everything. Why? Because if you want to succeed in being a gateway for others, you have to hone in on what matters to you more than anything.

This is where many people fail. They come up with a clever idea for a craft, a book, or a business, and they shove it into an otherwise crowded narrative. It's "in addition to," not a core part of what matters most to them. They fail because they care about this idea only insofar as it is clever and represents a lottery ticket in their life. They dream that if their idea takes off quickly, they will invest more of their life in it. What they are hoping for is that if they develop it just barely enough, others will come in and validate the idea, help it spread, and turn it into a movement. In other words, they want quick validation where others make the path to success easier for them.

This rarely happens. This is why millions of "clever ideas" sit on hard drives, in the bottom of someone's desk drawer, and in the back of someone's mind, never seeing the light of day. It is the reason why when someone has a huge smash hit with an idea, thousands of others say, "I thought of that years ago." Why did this one person succeed? Because they believed in it more. It was more core to their personal narrative of what mattered, and where they could devote their time, energy, and money. The person who succeeded waded through risk long after you would have said, "This is crazy … I'm not wading any further into this."

I want you to think about what you would fight to not lose. Those are your narratives. This is where you will put your energy every day, every week, and every month. It is where you will keep that flame alive long after others would have given up.

Too many people say they are writers, but never find the time to write. Or they have an idea for a sculpture, but keep delaying it until they clean out the guest bedroom to have the space for it. Or they are a musician who daydreams about creating music, but instead spends all of their spare time watching football. You are what you do, and when someone is as busy as you are, you have to be more self-aware of what that is each day. If you want people to make time to experience your creative vision, then you have to make time to create it.

Is there a disconnect between what you do every week versus what you want to be known for? Do you want to be known as a writer, but have struggled to write one thing? Do you want to be hired as a freelance writer, but don't write/publish for months — years even — because you are waiting for just the right opportunity? These are the difficult questions you have to ask yourself as you uncover the narratives that drive you.

Your narratives are two things:

1. The things in life that you care so much about that you would fight to protect them, and to ensure that they can reach their full potential. If they were threatened, you would risk so much to protect them — from not just physical harm, but even stature. You would gladly give up so much else to ensure these things continue to exist.

2. A practice. What you do every single day, every single week, every single month. Slowly, in small steps. You have to ask yourself: do you simply dream of moving ahead with your creative goals, or do you take action

on it? Are you full of hot air, even to yourself?

Here, we broaden your reasons for why you create. Your narrative is not just "I wrote this book about an underdog; I really hope this book finds an audience." Your narrative is, "I believe in the underdog, and in my life I champion and look out for those who have the odds stacked against them. I even wrote a novel about an underdog, and I think this story will inspire people to find the strength to not give up."

The first example is a product that you likely wouldn't fight to protect. Sure, you hope it works, you cared enough about it to create it, but if it failed to sell more than thirty books, you would likely drop it and move on to other things.

In contrast, the second example is a belief that is embodied in the book, but also extends beyond it. This is something you *would* fight for. Where, if the book failed to sell more than thirty copies, you move onto the next book about an underdog, or brainstorm other creative ways to help inspire others to find strength when they feel hopeless.

Be Clear About Your Priorities

Do this:

1. Take out a stack of index cards.
2. Spend fifteen minutes writing one thing on each card. Have it be a word or phrase of something that matters deeply to you, or that you feel responsible for. This should encapsulate your entire life, not just your writing goals. You may have cards that read "family," "take care of mom," "work out," "faith," take care of the house," "my job," or so much else.
3. Now, sit down on the floor or at a large empty table, and put the items that matter most to you at the top of a pyramid shaped design, and the items that mat-

ter less near the bottom. Place the top item in the pyramid flat on the table furthest away from you, and the lower priority items flat on the table closest to you. You will have three to six rows making up your pyramid, with one index card at the top level, two in the next, three in the next, four in the next, and so on.

In doing this, you may find that you start off with a square shape, with three or four index cards across the top, the middle, and the bottom. This is because it can feel impossibly difficult to choose a single priority above the others, especially when thinking about your entire life. You will have an urge to put "family" at the top, but then feel you also need to add "job" because you know that without it, you can't support your family. Here is an example of the shape you want to end up with:

The phrases in your pyramid will be different than those in the example above. When you create yours, keep in mind that no one else needs to see it, so play with putting different cards in different places. If, for a moment in time, you put "yoga" higher in the pyramid than "PTA," no one is judging you. In fact, I think it can be important to play with different orderings to envision the different ways you can structure your life, and force you to begin thinking about how to do what matters in your life when you have very limited time, energy, and resources. You may find that a goal such as "write my memoir" is such a burning desire that you can't help but put it very high in the pyramid. Or you may find that it is always secondary to so many other things.

The purpose of this exercise is to find clarity. It is also a way to find connections between the various aspects of your life. For instance, perhaps you are an accountant for a large corporation by day, and a mystery author by night. In establishing your priorities, these two are both near the top. Seeing that allows you to consider connections between them that you can use in your messaging when crafting your gateway. If you spent twelve years as an accountant, but are now writing murder mysteries, frame your accounting experience as teaching you the value of cold calculations in order to pull off the perfect murder.

Perhaps your day job has you doing a lot of travel to corporate offices all over the world. In connecting this to your writing, you can share photos of these places and interesting facts that would present you to the world as a mystery author who knows the ins and outs of glamorous and strange corners of the world because you are constantly traveling to them. Or perhaps you are able to consider how in your day job, people can hide secrets within the numbers on a spreadsheet. For instance, a company that hides enormous revenue losses via creative accounting. You realize that this is exactly what your protagonist does in your novels—they uncover nefarious dangers in our society that are hidden right in front of our eyes.

This exercise is about making choices about what you care most about, but also thinking about how you can use them to craft the narrative of who you are and what you believe. The gateway you craft begins with who you are.

Craft a Mission Statement

Let's craft a statement of intention, a "mission statement" if you will. We will continue with the same example of being a writer. The goal is to identify a simple sentence that focuses on the experience you want your writing to create for others. Please don't focus on the point of purchase—the marketing pitch as to why someone should buy your book. Instead, I want you to think about someone who purchased and read your book nine months ago. How do you hope it shifted the way they think? When do you hope they remember key scenes or characters?

This is where we bridge the gap between what writers often tell me and what I think they really want. Earlier in the book, I mentioned that oftentimes someone will tell me that the goal of their creative work is simply to "entertain people." Whenever I hear this, I don't think they are being honest with what they really hope. In truth, they are hiding behind a pithy statement. If you are merely "entertaining," then there is no need to have to consider what you or your work represents, and you are off the hook from figuring out how to best communicate that. But when you move past the idea of merely entertaining people, you are left to consider the gateway you are crafting. That can feel like a responsibility.

In nearly any book, TV show or movie that is popular, there are deeper reasons that people watch beyond being entertained. For instance:

When someone thinks of Jamie from *Outlander*, they are considering what it means to be in love with someone who has a deep sense of honor.

When they think of Tyler Durden from *Fight Club*, they are considering the other side of themselves that is bolder, brasher, more willing to take action.

When they think of Ned Stark from *A Game of Thrones*, they think of what it means to be the last holdout of family honor in an age of corruption.

Are these books entertaining escapism? Sure! But they are also so much more than that. When Diana Gabaldon leads us to the gate of *Outlander*, she is opening up a world to us. This is what Chuck Palahniuk does with *Fight Club*, what George R.R. Martin does with *A Game of Thrones* — what every author should do.

I use fiction examples on purpose, because I think it is a more difficult process for novelists. If you are a nonfiction writer or memoir writer, it is much easier for you to find that connection between the work itself and how you hope it affects the lives of readers.

Nine months after someone reads your book, what do you want them to think quietly in their heads about the world you have opened for them? How does it relate to their life, their identity, their interactions?

Stumped? Write down a series of belief statements — things that you feel resonate in your creative work. Sit with them for a week, reviewing them each day. Tape them to the wall the way you would tape different colored paint chips to the wall in a room you are thinking of painting. None may seem perfect, but at the end of the week, choose one that you are drawn to the most. Don't worry, just like paint, you can change it over time.

For example, this could be your mission statement: "I

believe that beauty exists in what we learn trying to connect our dreams to our realities." If you are a novelist, that may guide and explain a wide range of stories you craft about families who struggle, but are connected by a shared love and hope. If you are a photographer, that mission statement may guide you to travel the country to photograph people who are barely making ends meet, and capturing that vision in your photos. Or perhaps you are a songwriter; if so, that statement may guide five decades' worth of albums, countless tours, and periods of great success, and great disappointment. How so? Well, you may have noticed that my sample mission statement above is similar to one that Bruce Springsteen shared for his own work: "I have spent my life judging the distance between American reality and the American dream." That is a connecting thread between more than fifteen albums, 300 songs, and 2,000 live performances.

As you hone your own mission statement, go find the biggest magic marker you can, and write it in big letters on a piece of paper. Tape it to the wall next to where you write in your home. Now, take a picture of it with your phone. Go into your phone's settings and make it the wallpaper background to your "home" screen and "lock" screen. I want you to be reminded of your intention all day, every day.

We are building your gateway out of steel, not cardboard, and ensuring that you believe in your gateway with such clarity — such verve — that nothing can shake it.

Craft Your Bio

Start with your bio — the way you describe who you are and how your experience makes you the perfect person to write the books you are working on. Your bio may appear on the back of a book, but also on your website, in a query letter to an agent, or even in how you describe your work to someone you just met at a barbecue. Your bio should embody not just a chronological view of your life, but the narratives that fuel you. This is the first thing many creative professionals mess up. Let's talk about some common mistakes I see, and then some practical ways that you can use your bio to develop your narrative.

While there are many ways to craft your biography in order to communicate a narrative, this is a structure I often find helpful:

1. A belief statement that your ideal reader would read and say "YES! This!"
2. A description of the one thing you desperately want that reader to care about. (Hint: this should be your creative work.)
3. Your credentials as they relate to your creative work.
4. Your background and experience. Filter this through your creative work.
5. Who you are as a person. This is where your hobbies, where you live, and your background come in. Only *after* you have hooked us with the narratives that we care about.

Let's walk through each of these steps:

Bio Step #1: Start With a Belief Statement

Don't start your biography at the beginning of your life and work forward. Instead, start with the present and work backward. In other words, don't focus too much on place, without translating why this matters. Most people have pride in where they come from, and where they have lived. But what they don't understand is that their internal feeling of pride often doesn't translate into anything others can relate to.

It is a hollow stand-in for what we are trying to say, but aren't making enough effort. Am I proud to have lived in New Jersey my whole life? Sure. Some of that pride is just that — a personal pride that means nothing to you, since you are equally proud to have lived wherever you grew up. But if I tell you how proud I am of being from New Jersey, I'm usually using it as unclear shorthand for how I feel that represents me. I may be thinking "Being from New Jersey means that I'm a straight shooter, not easily fooled, and I come from a melting pot of different cultures and characters." But just saying "I'm from New Jersey" doesn't translate in that way to others.

Again and again, I have read biographies from authors that begin with something like "Born in New York, I spent my childhood in Arkansas, Montana and Oregon, before becoming an expat in Spain for several years as a young adult." I have no idea what they are trying to tell me here. These are names on a map, not a narrative. Can you include where you live (or have lived) in your bio? Sure. But don't start with it, end with it. That is information that is only interesting after you have engaged me with other things.

In fact, don't start with *you* at all. Instead, start with *me*. I know, this seems counterintuitive for a biography, but please hear me out. If you want me to pause from what I am doing to give you and your work a chance, you have to create a bridge. That bridge is from the things I desperately care about and engage with to what you and your work are about. This is why the first line of a book is so critical, or the beginning of any work of art. It serves to engage and communicate that the reader isn't wasting their time. If your goal is to have someone engage with you, you have to begin with empathy and start with *them*, not you.

This can take the form of a belief statement — the things that embody your work and your drive to create that would resonate with your ideal audience. This will be a version of the mission statement you crafted above. It can be what you are fighting for, or what you are fighting against. It can be a feeling that you want people to have when they experience your work. It can be a story that is shorthand for what your audience wants to align with.

Bio Step #2: Focus on Your Creative Work

Now that you have built a bridge from where your ideal audience is to what your work embodies, tell us about that work. There are two common mistakes I see people make at this stage. The first is (again), people start at the beginning and work their way forward. They tell the reader about their very first forays into their art or craft, and then walk us through it slowly working their way to the present. For a writer, they may present it as, "After receiving my MFA, I wrote a series of short stories before delving into my first novel." Then they list their first three novels before the setup to their recent shift to crafting a memoir. The problem? Instead of focusing my attention on the creative work that matters most to them right now, they require me to experience every step of the journey. That is a lot to ask up front. I mean, imagine meeting someone at a party and you ask, "So what do you do for a living," only to have the other person respond by reading off their resume, year by year. Bleh!

The second mistake people make in this section is to list too many things all at once, as if each has equal importance. They do so because they are trying to represent all of the nuances of what they love and are capable of. Again, if we stick with an author example, perhaps eighty-five percent of their focus right now is on their memoir which is going to be published soon. Instead of focusing only on that, they say something like, "Nature lover, author, accountant, painter and believer in all things that sparkle. Yankees fan."

Instead, I want you to slow down and focus first on the thing that matters to you in your creative work right now. If it is a memoir, take us through that. Spend two paragraphs on it, don't shove it into a list with five other things.

Bio Step #3: Your Credentials

This is where you build the case for why you are the perfect person to be creating the creative work you just described. Sometimes these credentials are achievements, such as degrees you have earned, or years you have spent in a specific field. But other times, they align to the narratives and stories we talked about earlier. This can take the form of a story as to how you got into your craft, or why it matters to you. For example, if you are crafting a memoir about surviving cancer, you can tell your own story a bit, or say things such as, "I have spent hundreds of hours volunteering with organizations which help those suffering with debilitating illness. I have sat by the bedside of more than three dozen women who were fighting for their lives, and losing. Their stories are infused in everything I share."

If you are an artist, perhaps you have no formal training, but you spent years visiting galleries in the city you live. Share that. If you are a musician, tell us about your passion, how you got into the style of music you play, your process, who inspires you. These may not seem like traditional credentials that appear on a resume, but they serve the same function; they tell the reader you are the real deal.

Bio Step #4: Your Background and Experience

This is where you can go broader into other areas of your life beyond your creative work: your career, schools you attended, achievements you have earned, and other skills you have. When sharing this, filter it through your creative work. This is where you tell us about your day job, but explain how it relates to the creative work you craft. For example, "Spending seventeen years as a carpenter, I learned that you measure twice, cut once. That is how I approach my writing, carefully crafting sentences that efficiently take the reader exactly where I want to take them."

Bio Step #5: Personal Details

While some personal details are infused in everything you would have shared in the previous steps, this is where you can place anything that didn't fit. Now you can tell us about the places you lived, if you love the Yankees, what kind of dog you have, or other hobbies. If you end with "I am the proud mother of three wonderful children," that doesn't mean that you put them last in terms of priority in your life.

Ending with the personal stuff allows me to connect with you as an individual after I understand the creative work that you want me to focus on more than anything.

Your bio is the centerpiece of the narrative that connects the work you create and who you are. Other ways to find your narrative? Consider what you *love* talking about. What topics could you sit at a cafe or bar and talk about for hours and hours? What types of people do you seek out and enjoy chatting with? I mean real people, not a mysterious and perfect "audience" that you imagine for your book. What are common traits of these people, what resonates with you about them, and they with you? What I want to encourage you to do now is find engaging ways to describe the practical things you already do, not write boring phrases that sound "professional" but are just safe ways to hide behind the same staid practices everyone else is using. For instance, I have read 1,000 LinkedIn summaries where people begin with "Detail-oriented team player seeks new challenge ..."

When you sound like everyone else, can you really be surprised that no one notices you?

Identifying your narratives and framing them into the context of your life through a biography is the first step, but now we have to dig deeper. This is the foundation for your gateway: to know what you stand for, and to share it in a way that truly speaks to others.

Craft Your Gateway

A gateway is not a business card, a clever pitch, or a website. It is how you craft and share your work with others, not how you schedule promotional status updates on social media that you broadcast out to "an audience." Your gateway is a process not unlike your creative work. You will hone it via habits, keen observation, and experimentation. Day by day, it will feel more true, as if it is the thing that people have been waiting to welcome into their lives.

Test Your Gateway

Analyze whether every aspect that surrounds your creative work embodies your mission statement. This begins with the creative work itself. Your mission can't just be a pie-in-the-sky hope for your work. It needs to reflect weekly actions you take to craft your work. In other words, are you a "working artist," a "working musician," a "working writer," a "working crafter"? If not, this is the place to begin. Craft your gateway by doing your creative work each week. This is perhaps the message you will hear repeated throughout this book most often. Again and again, I have met people who are frustrated that their creative work isn't connecting with others, and when I scratch the surface, I realize that they haven't created anything new in years. They are not a "working" artist, they are someone who created art three years ago, and are now simply trying to "sell" art. There is a difference.

If your mission is to "create music that inspires young women to believe in themselves," then the first step is to ensure you are creating this music each day, month, and year. You are what you do. Develop a simple personal habit of focusing on your creative work and how you share it with others. This is a critical distinction: you are not creating a product (a book, album, craft) that you are selling in a marketplace. That is simply a milestone. You are connecting other human beings to your stories and knowledge and, as a gateway, are opening them up to something new.

Consider how you do that every single day. You don't have to prove it to me, and you don't have to prove it to the world. Prove it to yourself. To track your progress of developing a daily habit, establish a system to recognize it. Create a journal where you update a simple daily log. Or post a calendar to your wall that you mark with a "check" if you attended to your creative work today. Or, simply take a photo of yourself each day when you are focusing on your creative work.

Be accountable to yourself before you ask others to validate and support you.

If you are like most people I know, you are swamped with important responsibilities. Schedule reminders in your calendar that help you to attend to your creative work, even if just for a moment each day. Here is the trick: if you are a writer, you don't have to write 1,000 words per day, or convince someone new to buy your book each day. Start with the smallest possible habit. Think of it as a single push-up.

This concept comes from B.J. Fogg, who does research on human behavior at Stanford University.[5] If you need to get in shape, you will have a lot of resistance — reasons that you can't find the time or energy or resources to do so. Instead, drop and do one push-up each day. That's all. No one can argue that they don't have time to do a single push-up. It takes less than five seconds, and can be done anywhere. This action developed a habit that will lead to your larger goal.

Identify the "single push-up" for your creative work each day.

Why are we doing this? Well, it is a "poseur test." I want you to confront whether you truly engage in your creative work as a practice and whether that strives to live up to your mission statement, or if you are just pretending to because it feels good to say so. Someone expressed it to me this way, "Everyone says they want to write a book, but no, they really don't. They don't want to do the work."

Now, I am not saying that you have to feel confident in your work, or that you need to prove that your creative intention lives up to your creative vision. I simply want you to ask yourself if you have a practice of creating your work that focuses on your mission. For example, if you are a painter who paints once per week, yet you feel like it is always crap — that counts! That is a creative practice that is the foundation of your gateway. If you are a writer who types 200 words a day that you struggle through and are embarrassed by — that counts!

Test and Hone Your Mission Statement

In the previous chapter, you got clear on your intention as it relates to your creative work, and how to communicate it. This will need to be updated and evolved, and I encourage you to *try* to break your mission statement. Why? Because too many people craft a half-way decent mission statement, then they cling to it. But just as your creative work does, it needs to grow and evolve.

Say your mission statement out loud. Does it sound weird?

If so, then craft a spoken version that aligns to the written version. Use it in casual conversations. For instance, when people you meet ask you what you do, instead of defaulting to your day job, previous career, or your role within your family, start by telling them your mission statement. This, "I am an artist—I create paintings that inspire people to look at the world differently," or "I am a novelist who explores how childhood trauma can help someone transform into a hero."

You can even seek out these conversations to test it. For instance, if you are that novelist, go to the library to find similar books. Go up to the librarian and say, "I wanted to know if you could help. I'm a novelist who writes about how childhood trauma can transform someone into a hero. I'm trying to find other books on a similar theme, can you help?" See how this feels to say it out loud to another person. Note where you lose them—where they don't understand, where it falls flat, and what their follow-up questions are. Use this to hone the language of your mission statement so that it is not only clear to you, but clear to others.

Believe in Yourself

I have met people who have published multiple books with large publishers, and still have trouble referring to themselves as a writer. For many, one of the most challenging aspects of this book will be to present themselves to others as an artist, a musician, a writer, a crafter, a photographer, or another creative professional. It is all too easy for negativity to cloud any positive feelings you have about your craft.

Even the smallest failure, a tiny amount of self-doubt, or the slightest critical comment by someone can kill your confidence and diminishes any momentum you have attained with your creative work. It is like adding a tiny drop of blue dye to a bowl of water. Immediately, all clarity is lost, and the entire bowl looks blue, even if the dye was only one part out of 1,000.

An artist I know recently told me this:

> *"The friend I got together with yesterday said*
> *something encouraging. She asked about my*
> *art with, 'So how is it going with your Etsy*
> *shop?' But this was followed immediately*
> *by something not as encouraging: 'Are you*
> *just gonna kind of leave it there and not do*
> *anything with it?' I explained why I haven't*
> *opened it up full bore with lots of prints*
> *because of the up-front cost, and how I am*
> *having to be patient. Later, in thinking about*
> *this, I felt challenged and affronted. I hate that*
> *she (and maybe others) is perceiving my Etsy*
> *shop as half-hearted. Her question is really*
> *discouraging to me."*

The artist, let's call her Stephanie, has been making incredible progress with her work and getting her shop set up. Yet, even a slight offhand comment can wipe away that progress, because it challenges how we perceive the value of our efforts. This is a pervasive roadblock for creative professionals.

I told Stephanie that her art becomes a mirror for those around her. That when her friend looks at the Etsy shop, she is not seeing art. Rather, she is seeing someone who is working to create something from nothing, to share their voice, and redefine how the world sees them. And that can be personally challenging to her friend. Simply by creating art and selling it, Stephanie can unknowingly challenge those around her to redefine how they see her and, because of the "mirror effect," how they see themselves.

When you follow your dreams, it can disrupt the world of those around you. You force them to confront their own barriers. They may have a creative dream that they haven't pursued. They may feel that they have good excuses as to why they haven't, and when you go ahead and pursue your dreams, it breaks their excuses. The easiest way for Stephanie's friend to cope with this is to try to put Stephanie back into the box — the role — that she knows her for, which is the always aspiring, never doing, artist.

I shared this story with some other writers and creative professionals, and they immediately shared their own versions of this story. I'm sure you likely have your own as well. Can you use this as motivation — turning negative energy into positive momentum? Yes. A sense of competition can be healthy, because it is a reminder to live up to your own goals. To be competitive with yourself. I also think it forces you to own your progress and double down on it.

I encouraged Stephanie to use her friend's comment as FUEL, and that the next time this happens, consider giving a response like this:

> *The friend: "How is your Etsy store going?"*

> *The artist: "Amazing! I posted a few pieces just to test it out, and made my first sale almost immediately. I'm learning all the ins and outs of printing, packaging, shipping, and customer service. I plan on adding 500% more of my art to the shop by the middle of the year — it feels incredible to finally be doing this."*

> **drops mic**

She replied, "Look at how much I've grown in the past twelve months. I began to take my art seriously and then I had people want to buy some pieces, and then I opened an Etsy shop and then I sold a piece. That's great! I'm making pretty fast progress, and I have a plan for making more progress. And I'm just going to take tiny steps forward until I'm posting and selling more work. I have a new goal in my plan: Have a 'mic drop' conversation at least five times in the next three months."

So much of success is about sheer persistence, and believing in yourself and your work.

As a creative professional, even though it shouldn't be, it is your job to reframe the conversations like the one Stephanie had with her friend. To turn negativity into positivity, even when the blue dye clouds your waters.

Create Mechanisms to Stay Motivated

We don't walk around pretending fires don't happen simply because we wish they wouldn't. This is why each floor of an office building has fire extinguishers, fire escapes, exit signs that stay lit even when the power goes out, safety procedures, a safety manager, and procedures to alert the fire, police, and first aid teams in the event of a fire.

When developing your creative vision, plan for disaster. Have mechanisms that are your version of "in case of emergency, break glass." This is for moments when you feel you are a fraud, that your writing is horrible, that you just can't find the time.

When you lose faith and clarity in your own vision and work, prepare a "reset" that reminds you of why you create. This could be a quote from your hero, a photo that sparks your imagination on what is possible, a biography or documentary about someone who inspires you, or a song that centers you. I find biographies of those who accomplished a lot are filled with reminders that it wasn't easy for them, but they succeeded by persevering through the down times. For instance, if a project I'm working on fails, I can remind myself that Walt Disney's first studio failed. It shut down, Walt let everyone go, and he had to pursue new avenues. His big success came years later. Too often, we streamline our perceptions of how others achieved success, and we assume our challenges are somehow bigger than they are.

Create check-ins in your calendar—daily, weekly, monthly, quarterly, yearly—where you write down the progress you have made. This is in contrast to how many people view their lives, focusing on all they didn't do in a given period of time. They are pulled down by an unending to-do list. Instead, I want you to recognize and honor the things you *do* accomplish. This could be a simple statement each day that you write down, "Today I _____, which made someone's day brighter." This prompt can be as specific to your creative work as you like, or you can keep it broad so that you always remember that even on days that you are drowning, you did something good.

Have an "emergency call" list of three people who motivate you. These should be individuals you trust, who believe in the possibility of what you want to create, and would take your call without judgment. That last one is a doozy, isn't it? Very often, our own internal fear of judgment will prevent us from reaching out to others for a moment of help. If you want to be successful in your creative work, you need to let go of that fear. You are creating work that matters. Don't let a fear of judgment keep your work from reaching the world. You can start this conversation with, "I just wanted to check in for a few minutes, I'm working on something that has me stumped." Make it quick and be clear—because this shows respect for the other person's time.

If you don't plan for failure, you will be shocked when failure happens, and unable to get back on track. Prepare now.

In this chapter, we framed how to craft your gateway. In the next two sections of the book, we focus on extending your gateway from something internal and personal, to something that others can share in one conversation, one interaction, one experience at a time. Let's open the gate and help people walk through it.

Section 2: Open the Gate

Bring People to the Gate

Too many people fail because they feel they can stop at this stage of their creative work. Many believe if they simply construct a gateway — defining their narrative and their creative work — people will come to it. They won't.

You can craft something truly magical, and hope people show up to experience it.

A book.
Art.
A song.
A website.
An Etsy store.
A business plan.
A social media account.
A performance.

But while your creative work may hold the potential to engage and inspire, its existence alone will not do anything to ensure people actually experience it.

I grew up as an artist. I went to a local art school starting at age five, and throughout my teens and twenties I created all kinds of projects: paintings, songs, pop-up books, magazines, photographs, poems, sculptures, movies, and so much else. I was the "art kid," and throughout my life, I have been surrounded by people who are pursuing their own creative work, such as dancers, actors, writers, musicians, photographers, videographers, and many others.

Countless times when I crafted my own work, or observed my friends doing so, I have seen a "great idea" developed, launched, and then flop. There are some common stages to this process:

- The passionate vision that drives the creator.
- The diligent execution where they create and complete the work they envision. This can be writing a book, creating a series of paintings, recording an album of music, etc. This nearly always requires working past boundaries, and feeling as though the creator has too few resources at their disposal.
- The hope around the launch, whether it is publishing a book, releasing an album, holding an exhibit, launching an online product/service, etc.

What follows when the creator shares their work with the world is often a sense of disappointment. Few people ever notice their work, it garners very few sales, and little attention. I have heard this again and again from people in a wide range of creative fields, and at all levels — from seasoned practitioners to those just starting out.

Sometimes the disappointment is mild; the creator appreciated the journey and feels satisfied that they finished their idea, even if few people ever discovered it. But other times, the disappointment is profound. During the process of preparing to share their work, the creator began banking on the hope that their idea would spread. They dreamt that when their work was released, a metaphorical gust of wind would come and take it and deliver it to others, whose lives would be changed by it. Their hope was that the same passion which created the work would somehow infect others. Its release into the world would not only bring joy to others, but validate the creator themselves and even shift their identity. Such validation would help them "escape" from a role that they may feel trapped in — the failed accountant, the nagging sister, the flaky artsy friend, the one who is always depressed, or so much else. The idea was that success with their creative work could make all of their past roles slip away and force the world to see them as the confident creative geniuses they aspired to be.

When this doesn't happen, the sense of failure can hit like a brick. They realize that their big idea fell flat, that they are trapped in the same old identity, and that their best effort wasn't good enough to reach a wide audience quickly. Too often, the effect of their work failing to reach an audience is that the creator stops. They never write another book, never produce another album, never do another series of paintings, or never get on stage again.

I am writing this book because I don't want this to happen to you.

Do I want you to be wildly successful with your creative work? Sure. But what I want more for you is that you keep sharing your voice and your vision with new work; that this work, over time, changes the lives of others for the better; that you concurrently develop slow organic growth, but also increase the chances of serendipitous luck that connects your work to even more people.

Where I feel people get off track is when they focus on numbers alone, forgetting about the importance of the effect of their work. They instead rely on stand-ins such as social media followers, downloads, awards, charts and data. They make an assumption that if 4,000 people downloaded their work, it must be having an impact, even if they are unsure of what it is.

The goal should not be data; the goal should be a

demonstrable impact that your work has had on someone's life. To experience this, you need to open the gateway you have built.

I will warn you, opening your gateway focuses on the aspect of life that most people are apprehensive about — being social. I'll walk you step by step through how to do this, and how to ensure it feels fulfilling. The goal is to ensure that your creative work truly reaches and engages others. If you feel your creative work is magic that will entrance others, you need to recognize that a spell book alone is useless without the skilled wizard or witch to bring those spells to life.

Opening the gate is about finding your people. Knowing what resonates with them, where they hang out, and who reaches them. Then, one by one, bringing them through the gate.

This is where people misunderstand the marketing and business side of creative work. They feel that if they create something compelling and then broadcast it to the world (too often by repeatedly sharing it on social media), people will come. In reality, how businesses tend to get started is by going out and finding those who may love their work, and engaging them one by one, directly. You must learn where these people hang out, what they need, what they love, how they like to engage, and then seek them out. It is active, not passive.

That sounds scary, right? The idea that you have to seek out your audience, one person at a time, and engage with them. Think of it as being back in high school — the same social fears we had back then still exist within us today. Maybe you remember that feeling of walking into the lunch room on the first day of school. You are holding a tray of fish sticks, and as you look out across the lunch room for a seat, you don't see any familiar faces. You panic, not knowing where to sit. If you sit in the wrong place, you could be rejected by others, or perhaps you will sit with the "wrong crowd" and forever be linked with them. Or worse, you sit alone, looking as though you have no friends as you dissect the fish sticks.

As adults, we have spent years developing a keen sense of how to create social safety in new situations. We often surround ourselves with safe validation. We stop going to new places and stop putting ourselves in new social contexts. We go to the same places to work and come home to the same family, because these things feel safe. When a successful vice president of a major corporation is invited to a party, she may have the same social fears she did as when she was thirteen and walking into the lunch room and not knowing anyone. That she is isolated and vulnerable. The fancy cocktail she is holding begins to taste just like a fish stick.

When it comes time to share our creative work, the high school fears rise up within us. It can feel like that first day all over again, where all of the security of friendships, sense of place, social standing, and validation are wiped away. We feel vulnerable because we are sharing something we care about with the world, and others can reject us. It is as if you walked into the lunch room, except instead of holding a tray of food, you are holding your creative work. As you look around the room, you are hoping for signs of someone noticing you and waving you over to their table—to be welcomed into a community of people who will appreciate what you have created.

Our social fears can cause us to resist reaching out to others as we prepare to share our creative work. We begin justifying that simply releasing the work should be enough to attract people to it. We hide behind romantic ideas that, "A creator doesn't worry about marketing; that would corrupt the work." Again and again, I hear creative professionals bemoan "the good old days" when authors and artists didn't have to worry about marketing.

This is a lie. It is an excuse to try to avoid the same

challenges that creative professionals have always had to face.

When you read about the publishing world in the '50s, '60s, '70s, and '80s, you realize that letters and lunches were a significant part of making connections to get one's work published or noticed. Marketing was about who you knew and the relationships you had. For instance, the art world was a community of relationships, and artists either engaged directly, or had agents/friends/spouses who engaged on their behalf. The music scene was forged by relationships of who knew who, and who showed up at the right shows night after night.

What you find is that if you dig into the story of someone's success "back in the day," you find a web of relationships, of persistent effort on the business/marketing side, and, of course, a lot of luck.

Everything about opening the gate is aligned to this.

The good news? It is much easier now to identify your ideal audience, connect with them, and share your creative work with them in a meaningful way. In previous decades you had to have access to the *right* people, and outside of them, you may have had very few other options to actually connect directly with your ideal audience. Today, that has shifted dramatically. You are no longer a struggling writer in 1972 with nothing but in-person meetings, letters which can take weeks to receive a reply, or the phone (with long-distance charges) at your disposal. You now have so many more communication channels, which can reach more people, more quickly, and in a more targeted way than ever before.

It's a great time to be a creator, because you can use all of this to your advantage. This work is about you taking nice small actions that are totally within your control. Instead of launching a "brand," you are simply seeking out small conversations, tiny ways of helping, and having meaningful conversations with people who will care about your vision.

This, as opposed to what so many people in our culture try to encourage you to do: go viral. Please take my advice and don't go viral.

Most people I know are introverts to some degree, and I find that social media and genuine one-to-one connections with others are actually helpful for introverts. But don't fear, you don't have to stand on a stage to pitch your ideas to thousands. This is about individual conversations, small moments, and a combination of sharing and helping, all filled with empathy. The payoff is that these things truly work to drive awareness of your creative work, and ensure it has an effect on the world.

That is what bringing people to the gate is about.

It's not about crafting the perfect Tweet that will skyrocket you from forty-two followers to 420,000.

Instead, you need to develop the skills that are universal and timeless to find your people, know what resonates, craft a connection, and help them to find alignment with your creative work. That process is exactly what I will walk you through in the next several chapters.

Success Comes From Mastering the Basics, Not a "Secret Formula"

A couple of years back, I was working from a cafe and overheard a conversation between two business professionals. It seemed the man ran his own business, a consulting practice of some sort. The woman asked, "How do you find your clients?" There was a hopeful tone; you could tell she was looking for a shortcut—a secret. As if she was expecting him to say, "I have found that there is this little-known tool within LinkedIn that delivers highly qualified leads," or he would say, "Overwhelmingly, I grow my client list by holding free workshops at local Rotary Clubs." Instead, he answered,

"Through a lot of hard work." His tone wasn't one of irony, or one of holding back. He sounded genuine, almost like he wished there was a better answer.

Whenever I see someone selling a success formula online, I think of this story. You know the kind of success formula I mean—pitching people on how they can find explosive success in audience size or revenue via some "secret" in Etsy, podcasts, webinars, courses, social media, or something else. Invariably, what people who sign up for these pitches are looking for is a shortcut, a "hack" that leads them to greater success with half the effort, in half the time.

What they ignore is the psychology of how success happens. Let's look at a traditional marketing funnel, which looks something like this:

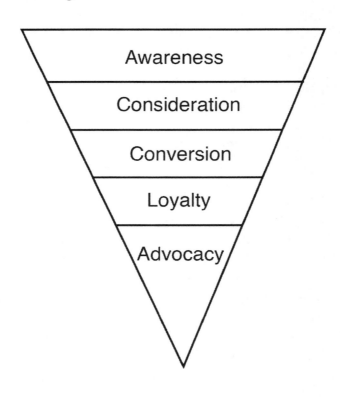

The top—the widest part of the inverted pyramid— represents the broadest possible message to the largest group of people. Each step down the funnel slowly leads those who are most interested in what you have to offer to deeper levels of engagement with you and your work.

Notice how the marketing funnel graphic has more than one step. Too often, people feel that to engage someone around their creative work, and perhaps make a sale, is a one-step process. They think that if they craft the perfect marketing message and post it in the right place, it will lead to sales. What you see here instead is that there are smaller steps leading to that type of engagement.

Another thing to consider is that the marketing funnel doesn't end with a sale. In this image, the sale happens mid-way down the funnel in the "conversion" layer. That term translates the moment when someone goes from being a potential buyer (or fan), to someone who takes an action to purchase your work (or follow you). For your creative work to grow, you have to envision the sale as one milestone in a much bigger process, one where people who buy from you tell others about your work. That is why there are two layers after "conversion," where people don't just buy your creative work, but love it, and seek out other work you create. Where they begin to tell others how wonderful you are and how they need to check out what you create.

How does this concept of a marketing funnel translate to a working artist? Often, getting a gallery show is something that happens after the artist has attended many exhibits at the gallery. It happens after they have understood and supported the gallery, the owner, and the community that surrounds it, and after dozens of conversations. A single pitch does not lead to a gallery show; instead, it is often the culmination of many smaller interactions.

When the artist does get a show, hoping people to show

up for the event is not a matter of assuming the gallery itself can drive interest. The artist invites their network and finds creative ways to identify who may want to attend the show. This is where knowing the narratives that drive your audience to take action comes into play. Use those deeper motivations when considering who would love to attend, and why.

For a creative professional selling their work, their biggest source of revenue is often repeat customers. Those who buy work from them again and again, and who encourage others to do so as well.

This process holds true for small businesses, and it was perhaps the most surprising thing to me about running my own. Despite reading so many books about what it takes to encourage growth via new customers, what I found was that I didn't need a huge email list and massive reach. Instead, a lot of my clients were repeat customers or came from word of mouth—happy customers telling others about my work. I didn't need to cold call 100 people a day. I didn't need to create elaborate pitches and slide decks to try to woo new customers. I never went viral, and didn't need to. It has been astounding how much success can come from a small group of advocates.

With nearly every single successful creative professional I have ever spoken to, I find their success comes from mastering the basics—the stuff about creative work and human nature that has been true for decades, perhaps even centuries. To begin, we will put your gateway into context; this is not an idealized scenario where vaguely defined people will follow a magical process to find your poorly communicated work. In the first section of this book, we began by focusing on the vision and passion you have in your heart and mind—the things that drive your creative vision. Now we will flip that and focus on those you hope to reach.

The first step is to find and explore the path that your

ideal audience already knows and walks along every day. The goal is to have empathy for who they are, what they already know, their habits, their interests, and who they trust. If you want people to find your gateway and walk through, you first have to walk a mile in their shoes. Doing so is about understanding them and their marketplace, and using that to hone how to communicate about the work you create. It helps you identify where you need to be, what engages others, and who you need to know. It also helps ensure that this is fun and meaningful for both you and them.

Instead of constructing your gateway out in the wilderness where there are no pre-existing paths, we are going to construct it closer to where your ideal audience already walks. Find the paths they know and love, so you can place your gateway in exactly the right spot. You are going to ensure the words you use to attract people to your gateway are understood by your ideal audience, engaging them and drawing them closer. Your work will speak to them when and where they need it; and when the moment is right, you can open the gate for them to pass through.

Avoid "Best Practices"

In order to identify what will engage your ideal audience, I encourage you to spend time doing primary research. Spend time "in the field" to learn about where these people are, who they are, and what engages them. All the while, take into account who you want to reach, your vision, and your goals. Primary research means figuring things out on your own. It goes deeper than reading a blog post with a headline such as, "10 Ways to Easily Sell 20,000 Copies of Your Work via Facebook!"

I have found that many creative professionals try to avoid doing primary research. Why? Because it sounds like work when compared to "best practices." If you're serious about building an audience for your creative work, skip the "best practices."

We believe that best practices are what we should seek because we want a shortcut. We want to know exactly what worked for others, and then (and we hate to admit this part) we do it half-baked. We want to see the 20 steps that worked for someone else, and, then do the eight steps that we are most comfortable with and can do most easily. We end up with a pathetic copy of a copy of a copy. Then we are disappointed when this doesn't lead to success. It's as if I gave someone a recipe for a great cake, and they only used four out of the twelve needed ingredients because that is all they had in the house.

Researching "best practices" is something we justify because we want to feel that we are preparing to do things smartly. The reality is that we are waiting until we feel less afraid, or the world makes it safer with established, accepted practices. We tell ourselves this research is to make "informed choices," so we delay action. But if you wait for it to be "safe," that means you are crossing the same street with thousands of others. The rush to "be the first to the other side" has long been won by someone else, and what we find on the other side is that it is crowded. You are merely one of the pack of people simply copying, and therefore receiving, almost none of the original value.

Instead, you are copying things that thousands of others are copying at the same time, which are often tactics that worked for someone else — once — two years ago, and now delivers a tiny fraction of the value it delivered that one time.

As I was writing this section, I took a break and checked Facebook. I saw an ad that illustrates this exact point. It said, "This email 2x'd our sales. Want to download 26 email scripts that will 2x your sales?" They are dangling a carrot, luring people into believing that a single tactic can double your revenue if you simply copy it. What is missing? The 1,000 steps they took before they sent this email script to their audience. How do I know that? Because the person who created the ad is someone I follow online, and I have listened to hours and hours of webinars, interviews, and online chats where he describes the many experiments he and his team did to find what works. They invested thousands of dollars and hundreds of hours to figure things out.

If I download his email script and send it to my list, I would be half-baking their strategy — at best. That person does so well in his business because he spends his days doing primary research on what works, instead of copying single tactics that others try to sell him.

Here is another "best practice" example from Joanna Penn, a very successful author I know. She shared a post where she described her experiment with "ad-stacking" to promote her books.[6] Unlike the previous example, her intention wasn't to persuade readers to try ad-stacking, she was simply sharing her experiences. If you know of Joanna and her accomplishments, you may be thinking, "Oh, Joanna is so successful and smart; she makes it look so easy. I should do ad-stacking too!" While she is indeed smart and successful, I would bet that it doesn't feel "easy" to her. Although she no doubt has pride in her accomplishments, she may be thinking, "Um, why is this such a struggle for me? Will ad-stacking even work? Why do I have to invest in an experiment that utilizes 10+ systems all at once and requires a $5,000 cash outlay?"

One thing I thought after reading her post was, "As usual, Joanna is awesome." But another thing I thought was, "Figuring out ad-stacking sounds like a huge pain in the butt." I imagine most authors would rather spend their time doing anything else than this primary research.

These are the services Joanna used in a coordinated fashion for a single promotion:

1. BookBub Featured Deal
2. BookBub Ads
3. Booksends
4. Just Kindle Books
5. Kindle Nation Daily
6. BooksButterfly
7. eReaderNewsToday
8. BargainBooksy
9. Facebook Ads
10. Nook merchandising
11. Amazon, email marketing, and podcasting

Joanna concluded that this promotion was worth doing, but it's worth noting these efforts weren't around a huge book launch. Instead, they brought incremental growth to an already fully functioning platform. While some would view her ad-stacking experiment as building a gateway, it isn't. Joanna is using it to reach an audience she had already identified and is leading them to her gateway which she set up a long time ago. She has thirteen novels, eight nonfiction books, a weekly podcast (with 283 published episodes), a blog/newsletter (published every month since December 2008), and other services around helping authors. In other words, the value she gleaned from ad-stacking was on top of the thousand other things she has been doing consistently for the better part of a decade or more.

Although Joanna was sharing her experience rather than trying to sell ad-stacking tips to naïve readers, there are plenty of writers who will read her post and try to half-bake it. They will try ad-stacking when they haven't setup the ecosystem of books that Joanna has already published. They will have one debut book with zero reviews, and try to copy Joanna's ad-stacking experiment as a way to find their audience. Or they may have a few books published, but they will only focus on choosing two of the ten ad networks she used in an effort to spend as little money as possible. They will cut corners on what Joanna did, and tell themselves, "Hey, if it only worked half as well, that would still be amazing." The truth is that in order to achieve the same results, they will have to work twenty times harder than Joanna, because she has a decade's head start on them.

Most people I know are overwhelmed by this type of secondary research. They have a never-ending pile of "best practices" to go through—hundreds of blog posts, webinars and courses, all of which are selling them tactics to copy. Every week I speak to a creative professional who bemoans "all the things expected of them." The problem? They are so busy chasing all of these "best practices" that they can never feel like they are developing meaningful practices that work for them, and grow over time.

I want to encourage you to do primary research in consistent and action-oriented ways. While there are many benefits, these two reasons are critical:

1. To truly understand who the ideal audience for your work is. Not in vague demographics, but because you have met them, and have a deep experience of understanding what engages them and why. You can put names and faces to them.
2. To develop colleagues—others who work in your field, support the type of creative work that you do, connect that work to an audience, and are advocates for it.

Whenever I meet a creative professional who truly feels lost in the marketplace, these two things are always missing. The result is that, without truly understanding their ideal audience, they are left chasing anyone who will listen. They begin copying copies of what others are copying because they feel so far removed from someone who may appreciate their work. They feel as if they are sending up little rockets to communicate to an alien race which lives on a distant planet. Each rocket contains some "best practice" idea that they heard about which will engage the aliens with their message. They shoot one up. Then another one with a different idea. Then another.

Meanwhile, billions of miles away, these rockets shoot across the sky of the alien planet—another mild distraction which doesn't fully engage the aliens in any way. Why? Because they are inundated by thousands of other rockets doing the same thing, vying for attention in the same crowded sky.

This is how your intended audience feels. They are overwhelmed managing their everyday lives, and are unlikely to make a purchase or become a raving fan because they saw a single Tweet, newsletter, video, or status update rush across their web browser. Doing primary research lays the foundation for capturing the attention of your ideal audience in a way that is sustainable and meaningful. It has many benefits, including:

- Telling you what your ideal audience cares about.
- Indicating where they hang out online and off.
- Hinting at what other creative work they love and why.
- Identifying who they admire and listen to.
- Being a process original to you.
- Allowing you to tap into and experience your creative vision in a fuller way.
- Helping you manage the complex emotions and psychological triggers around creating, sharing, and the business aspect of your work.

When you are done, you will have a sense of how to craft your messaging, where you need to be, and who can help connect you to these people you hope to engage. What's more, the process will align to and support your creative work, not get in the way and eclipse it. Doing this allows audience outreach to feel meaningful to you, where every time you learn something new about your audience, it fuels a deep sense of momentum.

Start With What You Know

Tennis legend Arthur Ashe once said, "To achieve greatness, start where you are, use what you have, do what you can." That is exactly what you are going to do to begin your primary research, focusing on learning about your ideal audience in the context of your personal creative vision. The process starts by exploring the ways that comparing your work to others actually helps you gain clarity.

Whenever I talk to someone who is mid-career about these steps I am about to take you through, they nearly always say, "I wish I would have done this work sooner." Why? Because too many creative professionals hope that they can skip this work and simply let the marketplace define their work for them. They want to release their work and passively hope that others take the effort to ensure it reaches their ideal audience. By positioning their work in a scattershot way, they give up months and years of learnings, and they risk their work never finding an audience. It's far better to know from the beginning why it resonates.

I call this process "finding landmarks." They are meant to help guide you from where you are to where your audience is. What I love about this system is that it works in both directions:

1. First you will use landmarks for you to move out-
   ward from where you are to understand the market-

place where your creative work will exist, and then, to find your ideal audience.

2. Then, we will reverse this, turning the same landmarks into guideposts to leave a trail for people to follow to lead them back to your gateway.

Landmarks are the examples of what you hope your creative work aspires to be like, which your ideal audience knows universally as the best example of the kind of work you do. What you want to do is not find landmarks *exactly* like your creative work, but instead focus on the positive emotions people feel about similar work already, and redirect those emotions and attention to your own creations.

What we are doing is identifying "comps," which some people describe as "comparable work" and others as "competitive work." They are the other things in the marketplace that your ideal audience likely already knows, and has some similarities to what you create and why they may love it.

Typically, you would describe this with a twist. Something like:

"My book is like Harry Potter, but with bakers, not wizards. It's about a kid who discovers she comes from a long line of expert bakers and is welcomed into a school for baking. But there is an evil woman who wants to steal all of the recipes and gain total baking power."

When thinking of this, I was mashing together Harry Potter and Strawberry Shortcake. Simply naming those titles brings to mind another way to use landmarks. "My book is like Harry Potter meets Strawberry Shortcake." Boom. If you are talking to a Gen Xer or even a Millennial, you now have them curious. That is the power of the landmark. It borrows the power of something your audience already knows and loves.

Don't think of this as a way to elevate your work. For

instance, a writer who says, "Oh, I write deep, multifaceted characters like Hemingway, with hyper-realistic situations like Tolstoy." I can't even tell you how many authors I have spoken to who tell me the only comps for their work are someone like Twain or Dickens or other classic authors.

This is where people go wrong. They are so obsessed with convincing other people that their idea is so amazing, if only they would give it a chance, that they are blinded by it. They feel they have no comps, that their work is so unique in the universe that it is incomparable. I call this the "special snowflake syndrome." I am always telling people that while they themselves are unique people, their creative work exists in a marketplace where their ideal audience is overwhelmed and is seeking out what they know they like.

They are mistaking what they hope their work becomes with practical ways in which others would consider landmarks as a way to find their work. Instead, flip it — consider how your audience reacts to the landmarks you identify, and how they can use those to become aware of yours. Use landmarks to help others navigate their way to your gateway.

While you can argue, "But Dan, no one knew that they needed *The Great Gatsby* before F. Scott Fitzgerald wrote it," I would say they did know that they liked rags to riches tales and stories of unrequited love. Does that mean Fitzgerald — or you — should write to the market? No. But you can be aware of the themes in your work that align with what readers love.

It's worth noting that our perception of Fitzgerald's book has changed over time. From Wikipedia: "First published by Scribner's in April 1925, *The Great Gatsby* received mixed reviews and sold poorly; in its first year, the book sold only 20,000 copies. Fitzgerald died in 1940, believing himself to be a failure and his work forgotten."[7]

Be the Gateway is about ensuring you don't die like Fitzgerald, never knowing your work mattered deeply to people. It is about you taking control to ensure it reaches the hearts and minds of people, not hoping that history reviews your work after you are gone. Even knowing you reached one person on a deep level can radically change the momentum for what you create. When you change someone's life with your creative work, you create an energy that tends to spread.

We will use comps to help you understand how your work fits into the lives of your ideal audience, how others would describe it, to use as a model for success, and to begin uncovering the path that leads to your gateway.

Find Five Comparable Works

You want to find five comparable works to your own. To be useful, they should have had some success, but if possible, not be the breakout hits that defined a generation. Sure, you can use one of those to get started, as we did above with the Harry Potter example, but here the goal is to learn from those who have found success you seek, but didn't have a "once in a generation" lightning strike. Comps should:

- Be released within the past one to five years. Older work had to compete in a different marketplace and is less useful for our purposes here. Also, it is too easy to cherry-pick classic work from decades ago that has stood the test of time and say, "That's like my work! Classic!"
- Have some level of public validation, such as reviews, media attention, an audience, distribution, etc.
- Be within the same field as the one where you create. In other words, don't say, "I am the Apple of pop-up books."

To find your comps, follow these steps:

1. Begin with Landmarks

If you are unsure of where to begin, start with the big prominent names in your field—the people who everyone knows. Go to the marketplaces where this work is shared or sold. I tend to find online marketplaces that offer customer/consumer feedback to be best, but I will include in-person options as well.

- For books online, go to Amazon or Goodreads. For physical books, go to libraries or bookstores.
- For art or crafts online, use Etsy, DeviantArt, or even Pinterest. For in-person, visit art galleries, museums, or specialty libraries.
- For music, check out SoundCloud, Spotify, or other online music communities.
- For photography, use sites such as Flickr, Etsy, or Instagram.
- For video, try YouTube.

Then, begin with the landmark in your field whose work you feel has some relation to yours. This is not you comparing quality; it is a matter of choosing the same type of story, song, image, etc. You can do this in three ways:

1. Based on your experience, you already know how you or others would identify similar work to what you have created.
2. Ask someone who has more experience than you do, like a librarian, a gallery owner, a radio DJ, etc.
3. In the online communities I mentioned above, study their category listings and look at the work that is displayed for each.

For example, if you wrote a memoir about discovering yourself, you could start with a landmark of *Eat, Pray, Love*. You may begin there because it is the only memoir you ever read, or it is the only popular memoir you have heard of. You could go to the library and ask the librarian about popular memoirs on a specific theme. Or you could simply ask about what memoirs are popular right now. You could browse Amazon memoir bestseller lists and categories.

The goal here is to choose something because this gives you a place to begin. This is the place where you will have to battle the "special snowflake syndrome" the most. Remember that this landmark exercise is not about defining who you are, but simply understanding how the marketplace categorizes work such as yours.

Too many people stop here with the landmarks. They say things such as, "My books are like those of David Sedaris." Or, "I want to be as big as Bruce Springsteen." Or, "My art is as challenging as Warhol's was." Don't confuse the effect you want for your work with how you understand the marketplace, or how it will define your work. I won't lie, I tend to find that people won't dig deeper because they don't want to see the reality of the marketplace. They instead want to envision comps at the shallowest level — only sticking to their inspirational heroes, because they cling to the narrative that the world will magically discover and celebrate their work. This allows them to avoid having to think about the marketplace or engage in developing an audience. They become so blinded by their dream of their creative work "hitting the lottery" that they forget to do the work they need for it to reach people.

When they scratch the surface, they are confronted with the idea that there are thousands of people producing work similar to theirs. Or that their work may simply find a place in the middle of the market — with forty reviews on Amazon, not 4,000; with 2,000 plays on SoundCloud, not two million. It can trigger all kinds of fear. People love to dream about their creative work as a lottery ticket. They will wake up one day to smashing success, and they themselves will be validated, their identity shifted in a compelling new way. It also confronts their own sense of identity when they realize that there is a universe of similar work.

This research will require you to be more open about your work, understanding the marketplace, and how you fit within it.

2. Find Guideposts

Now that we have identified landmarks, we have a place to begin. From here, we can find the people who have created similar work to you, finding success in the process, but perhaps haven't had massive breakout hits. Why do we lower our aim like this? Because we want more practical examples, instead of someone who won the lottery. One thousand women could write a memoir about hiking, but the success that Cheryl Strayed experienced with *Wild* would be singular. There wouldn't be a bell curve of how successful those 1,000 books would be, with Cheryl's book at the top, and then a gradual gradation of other books in terms of popularity. It would be Cheryl's book selling millions, and then the next closest "competitor" selling a couple thousand, and down from there.

Guideposts help you navigate the marketplace by understanding it better than most others. One by one, they guide you not just to where your work fits within the marketplace, but to the people who would love to hear about what you create.

This step is about the value of primary research. I'll stick with an example using books, although this process works in all marketplaces for all kinds of artistic endeavors. Go into Amazon and type in the names of the authors you have identified whose works are landmarks for you, or the names of specific books that you feel are guides. Now, scroll down to the "Customers Who Bought This Item Also Bought" section and click on each book. Keep scrolling to see all of the books Amazon displays here. Amazon provides similar features that may be useful, such as "What Other Items Do Customers Buy After Viewing This Item?", "Frequently Bought Together", and even "Sponsored Products Related To This Item."

As you review these other books, look for those that were published within the past five years, which have some reviews (at least twenty), and most importantly, that you feel resonate with the work you create in some way. None will be perfect. What you are seeking here are general categories and general alignments. Keep clicking on books and reading their descriptions. Keep seeing what categories these books are placed in within Amazon. Write down the names of the books and authors whose work resembles yours in some way; note why that is the case.

You may find after an hour of research that you keep running into the same books again and again on Amazon, and new books they display are in wildly different categories. Exhaust this avenue, then move onto the next step. The end goal is five comps.

3. Obsess About the Voice of the Reader

If you have felt a bit turned off by me talking about "understanding the marketplace," I can understand. For many creators, the marketplace is an unwelcome part of their creative work. Sure, that person wants success, but they fear catering too much to the marketplace, and may even be overwhelmed by the very idea of connecting commerce to their creative work. So let's shift our focus to the person you hope to reach with your work. We will continue with the example of books, so in this case we will be focused on readers. In other words, we are going to use these intermediaries, such as Amazon, to connect us to actual people and what they love about these books. If in the previous step you had asked a librarian about memoirs like *Eat, Pray, Love,* in this step you are asking them to put you in touch with five local readers who loved it. Then, you are going to talk to those five people.

Luckily, because of the Internet, you don't quite have to go that far just yet—reaching out to people you don't know; we can instead focus on reading the reviews people have left on Amazon. What we are most interested in here is understanding the voice of the reader. For the comps you have identified in the previous step, go to Amazon and begin reading through reviews. I would encourage you to read all of the reviews for each book. We want to know what readers liked about the book, what they didn't like, and why. Pay very close attention to the language they use. Look for trends in terms of phrases or focus.

For example, when I did this exercise for a historical fiction author I was working with, we began with Diana Gabaldon's book *Outlander*. This is a book that I would call a landmark for the historical fiction genre; it is wildly popular and highly respected. It seems to hit that sweet spot between historical accuracy and a compelling story that engrosses readers.

In studying the tens of thousands of reviews for *Outlander*, I began to notice a couple of trends:

- Many readers said they don't normally read romance novels, but they loved this one and its romance elements.
- Many readers only mentioned the historical accuracy as a secondary reason they liked the book. For

instance, if their review was three paragraphs long, they would talk about the story and romance in the first two paragraphs, with a single mention of the historical detail in the third paragraph.

Why are these things important? The first item illustrated that readers were sucked into story elements that they have resisted in the past. They seemed to take pride in never having read a romance novel before, almost as if they looked down on them. In the reviews, they encouraged other non-romance genre readers to give this book a try. The second item confronts a challenge that many historical fiction authors have, which is they are so enamored with all of the historical research they have done in writing the book that they want to put it all in because they feel it gives the book a sense of accuracy and weight. However, when you combine both of these points, you come to realize that what readers want is to be sucked into a story, not a history lesson, and they want to feel a human connection to the characters and contexts. For a writer who is more of a historian focused on details in history, this is a powerful lesson to learn. If they want to engage readers similar to Diane Gabaldon's, they should focus on engaging readers with the human side of their novels.

For each of the comps you find, identify how others categorize them. You can look at the Amazon category rankings for each book to see how the book is defined within Amazon. This gives you a sense of where it would be placed in a library or on the shelf of a bookstore. This addresses a soft spot for most creators — how to categorize one's work.

As someone with a personal vision, I imagine that you resist categorizing your own work. You don't want to be pigeonholed, or admit that your work is limited in terms of who it can affect, or the category it would do well in. At best, people will often mix categories. For example, imagine it is the early 1970s, you are George Lucas, and you have been crafting the screenplay for *Star Wars*. You meet someone at a party and they ask what you are working on, and you say, "It's a space opera — like an adventure thriller with romance theme, but also a story of hope." Why do you shove so much in this short description? Because simply saying "sci-fi" would negate the complexity of the story, the emotion, and how far-reaching the potential audience could be. When you said sci-fi in the early 1970s, you were talking about a fringe genre that spoke mostly to social outcasts. It was an out-of-style genre that harkened back to cheesy 1950s movies about aliens taking over the world.

Yet the marketplace always calls it sci-fi. It is a shorthand that doesn't explain the full depth of the work, but acts as a signal to those who may be interested in it. Bridge that gap for your own work — don't fight against how people want to talk about your work.

This brings us to my favorite part of Amazon — the search box within reader reviews. I love this tool! Let's say you are trying to determine if you should describe your book as a "psychological thriller" or "suspense." Or perhaps you are wading through thousands of reviews of comparable books, and trying to figure out what themes pop up again and again in reviews. This search box will help provide the data you need to decide.

After reading through the reviews of a comp, make note of phrases you see again and again, or phrases you are curious to see pop up. Then, type those into the search box and see which occur more frequently. If you are researching the readers of a comp and find that out of 1,000 reviews, only twenty mention the term "suspense," but 200 mention "psychological thriller," it gives you an idea of the terms actual readers use to define books such as yours.

In doing this exact research for a thriller author, I found that in comps, readers were obsessed about plots that kept them guessing until the end and had lots of twists. This helped us craft a book description based on what we knew readers were looking for.

This is not about writing to an audience, but understanding how the expectations and desires of a reader do and don't align to your work. It helps you better present your work to those people and understand why they read it, not just why you wrote it.

The three steps above begin the process of identifying how your work fits into the marketplace, and the expectations of those who you hope to engage. A few other ways you can begin this research:

- Review "best of" lists each year, but also user-generated lists that are created on sites, such as Amazon for authors and Etsy for artists and crafters. If you find an artist who feels like a comp, see how Etsy categorizes them. Then, explore other artists in that category.
- Review how the artist describes their work. Look for phrases that resonate. My gut feeling is that you will see common themes emerge.
- Do Google searches on the work that you do find, even on the most basic definitions of what that work is. Switch to a Google image search to see what comes up. Then do a Google video search. Don't stop at the first sign that validates what you already know. Challenge your assumptions, and move well beyond the first page of Google search results. If you want to truly understand how others will find and define your work and how it will fit into the marketplace, dig deeper than anyone else would.
- Look for mentions of these comps anywhere you can find it—blogs, podcasts, within major media, and well outside of it. Is it mentioned in a forum thread?

Find it!

Too many creators never understand the marketplace before they release their work into it. Why begin with such a handicap when there is so much research you can do from your home for free? Ignorance isn't an excuse for failure.

Befriend Guides

Now that you better understand the landscape and paths, it's time to find some guides—the people who can help direct other people toward your path. These are the individuals who have already engaged an audience similar to the one you want for your work. Their own work embodies similar things that yours does. For instance, if you wrote music, the guide would say, "Oh, I see you love MUSICIAN X; then you have to listen to MUSICIAN Y."

This work is different from finding comps because it is focused on the creators themselves, not just the creative work. This is the step that too many creative professionals miss. When someone wants to climb a big mountain, they likely prepare for months or years by studying maps, collecting equipment, and honing their climbing skills. While in many ways, they could be experts on that mountain, they may also hire guides to accompany them. These guides lead the climbers through aspects of the climb that you can't understand just by doing research.

For your creative work, you don't just want to have a map of your marketplace, you want to befriend those who have deep experience within it. Why? Because these people act like gravity to those you hope to engage with. They pull people closer to them with their work, their messaging, their events, and their network of colleagues.

You can think of this as market research, but it is squarely focused on people, the creative work itself.

1. Identify Mid-Level Doers

In the previous chapter, we discussed finding landmarks that your ideal audience knows. In some cases, this may include "classics" in your field. But now we want to turn our attention to what I call mid-level doers — those creative professionals who are mid-career, have found a sustainable way to focus on their creative work, and are a healthy mixture of aspirational and accessible.

- Aspirational. You aspire to be able to do what they do not just in terms of the work itself, but the lifestyle they get to live, or the validation they have received from others.
- Accessible. They are big enough to matter, but not so big that you can't connect with them. These are people whom you could reasonably receive a reply from if you email them. If you tried to meet them at an event they were holding, you would be able to do so.

Mid-level doers are those in your field who are showing up every day to create more work and connect with more people. If you want to see practical examples of how others define their creative work, craft messaging around it, and identify their audience, then connecting with mid-level doers is your best bet to find out. What I find is that mid-level doers are an under-appreciated resource in any creative field. You can begin with the comps you identified in the previous chapters — the people doing work similar to yours, but who have achieved a point of sustainability in their career. Don't treat other creators as "competition." View them instead as like-minded people who share the same passion that you do for this work and how it affects the world. Their experiences can shave years off your own journey in setting up your gateway and carving a path to it.

Look for those who are advocates for the type of work you do. This could be as formal as media (newspapers, bloggers, podcasters), but as informal as someone who runs a Tumblr or Instagram feed dedicated to the type of creative work you do. Who shows up to conferences or events, workshops, and online chats? Whom does your ideal audience already know and respect in their field? Make a list of potential mid-level doers to reach out to.

A particularly good place to find mid-level doers is podcasts in your field. The podcaster themselves is someone you should focus on because they have made it their job to understand people whose work resonates. The list of people interviewed is a great place to begin in identifying additional mid-level doers. If someone has been interviewed, that means they have achieved a level of success you can learn from.

2. Listen, Don't Broadcast

At this stage, too many people begin using social media to broadcast their creative work in the hopes that it magically finds an audience. Instead, I want you to do the opposite. I want you to think of social media as the greatest research tool ever created. This is a place for you to observe and listen intently, and in doing so, better understand the people who will walk through your gateway. Use social media as an input, not an output.

Find your mid-level doers on every social media channel you can. Usually, you can go to their website, and they will provide links to the social media they are active on. The first thing you are doing is noticing which channels seem to be more popular for your creative field. If your work is more visual, you may find Instagram a popular choice. For others, it will be Twitter, YouTube, Facebook, Snapchat, SoundCloud, or others. Observe which channels the mid-level doers are most active on, and have the most followers on, and then follow them there. Focusing is a big part of this. Someone may list five social networks on their website, but you should be able to identify the one or two that really matter to them. Focus on those. Don't just pick the network that you are most comfortable with — hone in on the one that *they* are most comfortable with. Many adults weren't comfortable with Instagram or Snapchat when it came out, because they mostly required you to use them on your phone; there wasn't a web interface. You may feel challenged even at this level — I don't ask that you feel comfortable in the process. I ask that you begin recognizing the practices that work for those in your field who are dedicated to reaching the audience you hope to engage.

You are following mid-level doers to see who they follow. Many social networks show this. On Twitter, when you click the "following" link for someone else's account, it shows you first the people they followed most recently. As you scroll down further, it will eventually show you the people they followed first.

See who these mid-level doers mention often in their social media feeds. Twitter shows this with the "replies" link, where it will show you their messages directed at specific people. But you can also observe any @names that the person mentions again and again in their feeds. Look for names and faces.

Then look at who follows these mid-level doers, but also see who mentions them, by searching their @name in the search field for each social network. This gives you a sense of who supports them, with names and faces, as well as their interests.

Give yourself a week or two, and simply listen. Look at every social media update they share. Don't look for a simple one-step marketing funnel, where a single Tweet leads to a sale or to going viral. Instead, focus on the people and what they engage with. Let go of your assumptions and your own narratives here. The guides you need to follow rely on these channels, and your ideal audience may love it.

3. Show Up, Observe, and Ask Questions

Show up to events, and instead of doing what everyone else does—glom onto the big stars and known people—focus your attention on the attendees. Talk to them. These events could be gallery openings, workshops, book signings, professional conferences, weekend retreats, concerts, craft fairs, studio visits, and so much else. Ask people why they came. Ask about what kind of work they love and why. Ask how they got into this field. Don't try to impress people, and don't try to sound too smart or savvy. Whatever you do, don't promote your own work. Simple questions to the right people almost give you a map to understanding the gateways that got these people into this type of creative work—and understanding their narratives.

I have a friend, Barbara Vey, who runs a blog and conference for romance and women's fiction books. She specifically focuses on readers, but in the process, she has become friends with hundreds of prominent authors, and has connections at most of the major publishers. Barbara is from Milwaukee and has this lovely way of tapping into the passion of why people read. Anywhere she goes, she asks people around her what they like to read. She would tell me stories of when she was in the hospital, and how she engaged all the nurses and doctors into conversations around books by asking this question.

Once I was on a very crowded New York City subway with her. I was dumbfounded when she struck up a conversation with a young woman sitting next to her and asked her all about what she liked to read and why. You see, on the NYC subways, you don't strike up conversations with strangers. Usually the mood is one of survival, not camaraderie. To my disbelief, the woman and Barbara had an amazing conversation, all while I was standing there, shaking my head.

I have met too many creative professionals who tell me that they don't have access to others in their field and so can't connect with their audience. Barbara Vey proves to me — and to you — that this conclusion is incorrect. It turns out that everywhere you go — the hospital, the subway — are opportunities for you to understand why people engage with creative work similar to your own. Do so by tapping into their passion, their reason for caring about it.

The key is asking. If you are unsure whether the book you are writing is considered to be in the Young Adult genre, go to four local libraries and ask the librarians about how they define YA. Do the same at any local booksellers. If you don't live near booksellers, pick up the phone and call some. Will the first five you call tell you they are too busy or give you a flippant answer? Perhaps. After all, booksellers are busy. But the sixth one may give you the answer you have been seeking.

Likewise, consider reaching out to those mid-level doers you identified. Ask simple questions that you need help with. Perhaps it is how that person got started; perhaps you are struggling with something. Be honest with them — don't try to convince them of how important you are, and don't tell them your life story. Ask a simple question in a grateful manner.

4. Focus on the People Behind the Brands

If there are brands or media that you feel your audience knows and respects, I would encourage you to not think of them as publicity channels for your work, but instead as people with a shared passion. A magazine is made up of individuals; it is not some monolithic entity. It is the same with any company or organization that you want to better understand or feel connected to.

Learn how the organization is structured, how many people are within it, and where they are located. For your specific field, see if there is a subgroup that specializes in it. For a magazine, you can start with the masthead printed in each issue, and then move to Google from there. Search the names of people who cover your field. Read their bios, see what they look like, and understand them as a person as best you can. See if they have social media channels they update. Look not just for updates about the topic you are interested in, but what else that person likes.

Why do this? Because more often than people would like to admit, who you know will help drive your career forward. When you see an author or artist in a magazine, the story behind how they got there is often about relationships. Someone pitched someone; someone knew someone; someone fit a need or preference that a specific editor had. Stop pitching blindly to "entities" and start understanding these organizations as real groups of multifaceted people, who are just like you.

One example of how to identify the people behind the brands in publishing is an email newsletter I subscribe to called Publishers Lunch. While it focuses on news and deals within the publishing industry, the most interesting part to me is the "People" section. They tell you about people moving in and out of companies. If you want to have a better sense of how marketing works within a big publisher, look these people up on LinkedIn. No, don't stalk them, and no, don't bug them. Simply do research to see what these departments and individuals truly look like. You may be surprised to learn that a specific organization has a single publicist and a marketing team of two. That could help you set your expectations for how much individualized attention you would get from them.

Too often, a single individual at an organization will become the "face" of it; I would encourage you to focus on the many others who show up there every day. These people are wonderful resources because they care deeply about work similar to yours. I find that too often, someone will seek out the bookstore owner instead of befriending the employee; seek out a gallery owner instead of getting to know the woman at the front desk; or send pitches to an organization, but never show up to events they run.

Bestselling author Thomas Greanias told me how, before he found success, he would drive to every bookstore he could find up and down the entire coast of California. He slowly built relationships along the way, and came to better understand the needs and preferences of bookstores. What's more, he knew their faces, names, and personalities, not a vague notion of what booksellers did and why. Perhaps just as important, they knew his. This allowed him to gain a keen understanding of how to position and market his books.

5. Use the Least Crowded Channel

Don't be a wallflower. Find the least crowded channel. Sometimes that is email. Instead of being the 20th person to go up to a gallery owner on the night of the big show, be the only person to show up on a quiet day between shows.

Send an email to mid-level doers instead of being the 80th person to come up to them after they speak at a conference. Look for the people who surround the mid-level doer, such as a manager, an assistant, the support staff. If you are attending an event that one of your heroes is putting on, befriend all the people who are working on it.

I did this with a meetup with Darren Rowse, a prominent

blogger who has developed a huge audience and earned millions with his own blogs. He lives in Australia and was visiting New York City, where the meetup was held in a bar. Everyone was crowded around him, vying for his attention. Those who weren't were "networking" with each other, exchanging business cards, and trying to impress each other with their big ideas. Now, I am an introvert. The idea of walking into a bar alone and going to a meetup group is basically terrifying. Usually, I go, make "an appearance," and count down the moments until I can sneak out.

But that night, I looked around the room to find someone who felt as lost as I did. I found a woman at a table where they had organized some of Darren's materials. I began speaking to her, and it turned out she had an Australian accent just like Darren's. It was his wife. I didn't ask her about blogging or the event; I asked about what I felt she would really care about: how was she liking NYC? What had they seen so far and what did they want to see? We chatted for a while, and I learned, to my dismay, that they were staying at a hotel in midtown, and other than Times Square they hadn't seen much. I offered to come into the city two days later, and have my wife and I show her and her family around. She and Darren were traveling with their first child at the time, who was still very young.

In the end, I was able to spend an entire day with Darren and his family, talking about all kinds of personal and professional things. My wife and I took them through Greenwich Village; we found the one store in the city that Darren's wife was hoping to go to, and crafted an experience that was genuine and wonderful.

Everyone else came to the meetup with a pitch to further their work. I went and asked someone who looked alone how I could help. The result was huge. The next time Darren came to New York City, we met up again. To this day, I am sure he and his wife will still remember that day in the city, whereas he may not remember a single person or conversation from the crowded meetup. Helping lasts.

Since I am an introvert, it was easier for me to talk to the only other person in the room that looked as alone as I felt. This is exactly what bestselling author John Green did back in 2009 when he attended his first event in the Harry Potter community. Yes, there is a Harry Potter community, and they hold an enormous event each year. Even though at the time, John was well-known, if not yet super famous, he considers himself an introvert. In the large convention hall, he hung on the edge of the back of the room — quite literally the definition of a wallflower. There he struck up a conversation with someone else who looked equally as uncomfortable; her name was Esther Earl, and they hit it off. A friendship formed, during which John learned about her battle with cancer.[8]

As John's own popularity grew, he came to champion helping others who had cancer, and brought Esther's story to the world. Hundreds of thousands of people who are fans of John became fans of Esther's, too, supporting her and others who go through cancer. All of this was because John was an introvert, and he simply found the least crowded channel to engage with others.

If you feel like an outsider to the community you hope to engage, don't let that stop you. One of my all-time favorite examples of this is Brandon Stanton. He grew up in Georgia, and when he was twenty-six, while working as a bond trader in Chicago, he bought a camera. He began taking photos of people in the streets on the weekend, and when he lost his job, he moved to New York City. There he started a blog, and as he continued taking photographs of people he saw on the street, he began asking them questions and sharing the answers.

With zero professional training or connections, Brandon

now reaches nearly 20 million fans on Facebook, more than 6 million fans on Instagram, and is the author of three books. You may have heard of his work — Humans of New York. All he did was ask someone on the street if he could take their photo and then asked them a question. It was so simple, yet his vision and drive turned the idea into something deeply meaningful for millions.[9]

It is also a reminder that there are stories all around us, waiting to be told. Too often, we miss them because we are afraid to ask — afraid of that moment of awkwardness and the risk of rejection. I encourage you to take that risk.

6. Interview People

Just as stories are all around us, so are the answers you seek about how you can craft and lead people to your gateway. Not by vying to be the billionth person to try to get the attention of an "influencer," but by interviewing the mid-level doers, the members of the communities you hope to engage, and the people who are fans of work similar to yours. Don't just follow others on social media — reach out to them. Ask questions and consider doing interviews. I have set up a blog post or podcast episode many times to offer the interviewee some kind of "promotion" for their efforts.

You can do this via email (send questions, receive back answers), Skype for an online video interview, phone, or meet in person. You can ask other creative professionals about their experiences at book readings; ask about their ten biggest fans; ask about experiences with those who buy their work, what drives them to create, and what is their process to create.

Interviews are an incredible way to gain access to those who would otherwise be out of reach. When I was in my twenties, I started a music fanzine — a self-published magazine focused on music and artists I liked. I had learned that if you said you were a member of the press, record companies would send you free CDs, so I began calling record labels and developing relationships. One day, while talking to a publicist about an upcoming album from one of my favorite bands, he asked, "Would you like to interview them?" I was speechless. I had never before considered it possible to meet these artists. Of course I said, "Yes," and then began calling other labels to ask to interview other bands I adored. What I discovered was that as a regular "fan," these labels had no reason to give me access. But as Press, I offered them publicity, and the doors suddenly swung open to let me in.

Interviews also help you to develop relationships and grow your own stature within a community. When I began my company, I became known to people because I interviewed others who did work similar to my own.

I have had clients who are breaking into new fields by interviewing people within them, and in a very short period of time, they have a wide range of relationships with insiders, as well as the knowledge those people have shared.

This isn't always only about gaining access to prominent people; it also helps you understand the needs of your community. In a previous corporate job, I was in charge of the company intranet — the internal website just for employees. To understand the needs of regular employees, I began doing two things:

1. Walking around different floors of our building and striking up conversations with people in different departments. I will admit that sometimes it felt uncomfortable, as if I'd walked into someone else's home. But I found that if you just casually walk through a few times, you become a familiar face. Then one day, you are in a situation to say something about the weather. Then on another day, you can ask them

a question. Before you know it, you have access. I am friends with many of these people years later on social media because of this.

2. I conducted formal interviews. As part of an intranet redesign process, I scheduled time for research. I interviewed more than a dozen employees in different departments about their work, their needs from my department, their work process, etc. These were all people I barely knew when I asked them if they could spare thirty minutes for the interview. At the end of one of these interviews, I thanked the person, and he said, "Thank you Dan. You know, I have been here for eight years, and no one has ever asked my opinion about things like this." Don't assume that by asking people questions, you are bugging them. People enjoy being asked their opinion, especially if they feel it could help others or create a change they would like to see.

Through this process you are creating maps. You are learning the existing paths, the people you need to know, the language your audience understands, and how to use that to connect your work to your ideal audience. Unlike the first chapter, this one is about other people. If you want to find success, you will find that empathy is a huge theme. The people I see who find success are masters at putting in the time to understand the communities they hope to be a part of. The core focus here is to consider the people who make up these communities, and create relationships with them.

Consider not how you can gain the attention of others, but how you can bring joy to them, and develop meaningful connections over time, because what lasts is what you create, not what you react to. It is the experiences you share and what you attend to each day, with the care of an artisan. The good stuff is created slowly, even as you struggle through the boring parts.

Creating your work — your writing, your art, your craft — and connecting it to the world is not just about the act of putting a product out there and publicizing it. It is about providing a gateway for others, being someone who is there when they need to experience joy, when they need to learn, when they need a helping hand, and when they simply need to know that there is hope.

What lasts isn't instant success, but that inclination to be present for others. That is what it means to open a gateway for them. Before we help others move through your gateway, we have one more step to take: to open the gate.

Open the Gate

As you reach this section, you may feel that this all sounds like a lot of work. As a creator, you may want to say, "But Dan, shouldn't my work speak for itself? Like the first time the world heard Elvis; the first time someone saw a Monet painting; the first time someone read Tolkien; the first time someone saw Fred Astaire dance."

I will admit—I love that romantic fantasy. But after working with so many creative professionals, I see it as exactly that—a romantic fantasy. That is the kind of thing amateurs who don't want to do the work of professionals tell themselves in order to let themselves off the hook. When I go to Spotify and see thirty million songs, go to Etsy and see more than one million people selling crafts,[10] go to Amazon and see more than thirty million books available,[11] or go to the Sundance Film Festival and see more than 4,000 feature-length movies and 9,000 short films submitted each year,[12] I remember the difference between the romantic fantasy of hoping the work will speak for itself, and the professionals who exhaust all avenues to develop a meaningful connection to their audience. It's like the difference between someone who builds a gateway versus someone who builds a house deep in the woods, hoping other people invest the time and money to bulldoze brand new trails to try and find it.

Back in 2013, Spotify released data indicating that four

million songs have never been played even once by a single user. That was when the service was five years old and already had twenty-four million active users. Many people feel that simply by releasing their music, it will go viral. All too often, their work goes unheard.[13]

Now, we take what we have found in this research, and we marry it to everything you crafted about your narrative and your gateway in the first section of this book. Let's now look at how you use your research.

The Channels You Should Use to Reach Your Audience

When choosing the channels you invest in to reach your audience, it should be a mixture of online and offline channels, which may include a website, blog, podcast, articles, email newsletters, print media (newspapers, magazines), radio, TV, and of course, social media channels such as Twitter, Facebook, Instagram, Snapchat, YouTube, and others.

Often in this book I will encourage you to ignore or challenge "best practices." What I mean by this is copying for the sake of copying, with the hope that it leads to a shortcut for success. But here, you want to use your research to determine the channels where your ideal audience is most engaged. You do not have to choose one strategy or the other—popular channels where your audience engages versus "the least crowded channel." You should instead use both strategies in different ways, at different times.

If you are creating a website for yourself, do a survey of ten colleagues to see what their sites look like. Then, for your own, I would encourage you to keep it as simple as possible in terms of both content and design. I have seen far too many people waste months of time trying to get their website to visually represent their identity. Don't. Your website is not you, and when you first begin, consider the most basic things it must do. Perhaps it simply functions as a business card, directing people to your various social media channels, and including a short bio. Perhaps it is a blog, or something larger.

If you spend months designing a website as a destination, you will likely be disappointed when you launch and few people come. Instead, identify the core things it has to do and include only those. Include as few items on the navigation bar as possible; write in the first person and not in the third person to directly address those who do come; and please, don't pretend that your website is a newspaper that has to have dozens of items to try to engage your audience. Focus their attention, and focus your own goals.

If you have multiple "brands" to manage, you have to consider if you need more than one website or if they complement each other. For instance, if you are an author who writes both children's books and erotica, you will need two different websites. But if you are a musician who also writes, you may be able to align both within a single website. Simply be aware whether you are focusing your audience's attention, or splitting it. It is difficult to be a gateway if you are showing people 100 smaller gates right up front, each leading to 100 different options. Be clear about what the main gateway represents, and why they would want to enter.

Consider whether you will create long-form content. This can be in text via blogs or articles, audio via podcasts, a music service such as Bandcamp or SoundCloud, or video on YouTube. This content can be unique from your creative work itself. An example would be a stand-up comic who also has a podcast where they interview other comics and deconstruct how comedy works.

Email newsletters are a way to directly reach out to those who want to hear from you. Consider the difference between a blog and an email newsletter as "pull" versus "push." With "pull," you are hoping to pull your audience back to your blog again and again. You are relying on them remembering to come back via a bookmark, RSS feed, or some other manner. When blogs first began, people would indeed develop those habits. But once social media became popular, people became overwhelmed with the firehose of content being pointed at them on Twitter, Facebook, and elsewhere. They would seek out blogs less frequently and rely instead on social media updates.

This is why email newsletters are a nice way to "push" your content out to those who choose to receive it. They receive an email the exact moment you want them to, and they can choose whether to look at it or not. Has email become an incredibly crowded channel where many others are vying for attention? Yes. But email still works, and for businesses, email converts — meaning that many brands rely on email to drive a huge portion of their business.

Social media channels can be used for many things. You can share your content, aggregate content from others, post status updates on what you are doing (professionally or personally) and, of course, directly engage with others.

This is not to say that you should simply think of social media as publicity. Too many people fail at social media because they immediately want to spread their message and ensure it is heard. Think about it this way. You walk into a party, and everyone is meeting new people and engaging in conversation. Perhaps you are a photographer and are always on the lookout for new clients — someone who is about to have a baby and may want to book a shoot with you after the birth. So you engage in meaningful conversations, but in the back of your mind, make a note of anyone who says they are expecting. Perhaps you follow up with them before you leave the party, just letting them know about your photography.

Then, someone new walks into the room and announces over the music, "Hey everybody, I'm Frank. If you are about to have a kid, talk to me about my amazing photography package. I brought handouts to show you my work, and please sign up here to get on my newsletter list...."

It kills the mood, right? You only see Frank as someone who is here for his own needs, and he is ruining everyone else's nice time because of it.

When it comes to social media, don't be Frank. Don't just constantly share updates about your services and intrude on others' lives. Instead, use social media meaningfully. Engage in real conversations, showcase your purpose and your process, and celebrate others who care about the same type of work you do.

Do you need to use any of these channels? No. You can be a successful creative professional without "needing" to do any of these. Some of you may have opinions about channels that don't work, with what you feel are well-considered reasons as to why. You will tell me a story of someone who tried Twitter and ended up getting trolled; or someone who invested a lot in YouTube, and it went nowhere; or how you tried Instagram and found it was all photos of what people were eating for lunch. The goal of research is to challenge your assumptions. Can you be contrarian and say, "Dan, social media doesn't work for my field, therefore I am ignoring it"? Sure. But if you are going to be contrarian, all I ask is that you do it with vigor. Don't be a contrarian as a way to get out of doing work, but as a way to *focus* your work. For example, let's say you reject the idea of using Instagram to connect with your ideal audience, even if everyone else in your field seems to use it. That is fine. But identify what you replace it with. How do you meaningfully share and connect with those people you hope to reach? Perhaps you instead want to send out handcrafted, printed fanzines (little magazines that are printed at home or a copy store). That's great! Do it all the way — do it better than anyone.

The Messaging That Represents Your Voice

Remember what we covered in the first section of this book—identifying your narrative as the foundation for your gateway? Now we combine that into all of the messaging you share with others, be it your biography on your website, or a simple status update on Twitter.

Often you will hear people say "be authentic" on social media, but I think that needs some clarification. Every day, before you walk out of the house, you put on a filter. This is present in the clothes you wear, how you wear them, your hair, makeup, the way you walk, the way you speak to others, and what you say. Likely, you don't walk around in your pajamas even if they are the most comfortable clothes you own. When someone says hello, you pleasantly say hello back, or say, "How are you?" even if you don't really want to know the answer. You do this on days where you feel awesome, but also on days when perhaps you feel the world is crashing down around you.

This is a filter. You are measuring what you share and what you don't, and how you do so. Doing so with your gateway is similar—honing the channels, messaging, and manner by which you share and engage with others.

Yes, you can focus on topics that you uncovered in the research earlier in this chapter, but also focus on the *feelings* that you give people. This is something that people who are amazing on social media do well, especially those who seem to "break the rules." They understand the feelings people want to have by following them, and they are able to be inventive about doing so. Communicating the power of your creative work is something your gateway provides.

To have people understand your work, you will need to become a student of those you hope to reach. This is not about writing to an audience, but simply understanding what works when communicating and what doesn't. Too often, we choose to communicate less as a way to mitigate risk in interpersonal communication. We stick to safer topics, we say less, we avoid new social situations, and never venture from the people and contexts we know.

When sharing the message of your gateway, be curious about other people. Generosity — with your time and attention, your talent and your enthusiasm — is a core way to engage others. If you do something such as an email newsletter, use it to tell other people's stories as it relates to your vision, not just your own experience. Being the gateway means that you are not sharing the same TED talk that thousands of others have, but instead, you are telling stories that are hidden gems.

Invite People to Engage

Too often, people assume that if they simply share good content, others will take actions on their own. For example, if you write a blog post, someone who enjoys it will share it with someone they know without you asking. While this does happen, sometimes people need encouragement, and need for you to give them permission and make it easy. In other words, consider the variety of actions you want people to take, and how that relates to your gateway.

If you have a single product to sell and feel that luring others to buy it is your gateway, it isn't. A gateway is not a clever pitch to buy a product. Musician and artist Brian Eno put it this way:

"Stop thinking about art works as objects, and start thinking about them as triggers for experiences."

Consider the variety of actions people can engage in that leads them to, and through, your gateway. All of this creates an experience that captures your ideal audience, and inspires them to create word-of-mouth marketing. What is the easy "way in" to your gateway? For instance, assume you are walking by a storefront, and perhaps the store owner has a desire for you to become a lifelong customer. Do they do a "hard sell" by putting someone on the street to tell you about how great their wares are? They could, but I imagine this would repel you from walking in. You would likely see them as an interruption in your day, pressuring you to give them your money. It feels more like a robbery or high-pressure negotiation, which isn't what you were looking for.

Compare that to a store offering a variety of ways to engage, and doing so in a generous manner. Let's use a yarn store, for example. They could offer a free workshop, a small craft for kids, cider and scones, a knitting group to sit in on, an exhibit of items made by local artisans, and so on. Each of these things is inviting, and it allows you a way in without feeling obligated. Consider how people engage with you beyond buying your stuff. What actions can they take after they buy your stuff?

You have built your gateway. You have forged a path to it, learned about those who will be walking that path, befriended guides who can lead them there, and opened your gate. Now, we walk people through the gateway.

Section 3: Walk People Through the Gate

Share the Journey

Don't wait for people to find and walk through your gateway on their own. Instead, one by one, bring people to your gateway and assist them in walking through it. To me, this idea is what separates those who dream from those who take action. Would it be nice to "go viral" and have people discover and walk through your gateway on their own? Yes it would, but that is not how we begin. Whenever I see someone who has tried and failed to engage others, it is often because they waited for these people to come, without seeking them out and helping them walk through their gateway.

This is not about your "hacking a marketing funnel," a term in various online promotions, which is meant to make you feel that there is a turnkey system that you can buy, and then find a shortcut for. Wouldn't it be nice to just drive down to the Dollar Store and pick up an audience, on sale, sitting right there on the shelf waiting for you? Engaging others is an inherently human process, one that is about connecting your work to people in a meaningful way, not using sales trickery. Your goal is not to be a street hustler, distracting someone with a magic trick so that before they know it, you've swindled them into buying something from you. When you build your gateway and walk someone through it, you are creating a fulfilling experience that provides long-term value.

The process of walking people through the gate is similar to how someone will experience your work. They measure the value not in the transaction of purchasing it, but in the experience of making it a part of their life. You crafted it with a vision, and they integrate it into their life in a way that extends that creative process. Perhaps you wrote a song about a relationship you regret, and someone listens to that song on a long drive after a relationship ends, and it gives them a sense of solace and hope; or you created a painting with a quote that inspires you, and someone hangs it next to the mirror they see first thing in the morning so they can be reminded to start their day with inspiration; or you wrote a novel whose main character had to sacrifice something important in order to help someone close to them, and someone who reads this book thinks about it as they work a double shift to support their family.

In other words, walking someone through your gate should not feel as though you have now become a "marketer" instead of a creator. It is about extending the experience of your creative work to at least one person in a meaningful way.

Communicating Your Journey

The act of creation is sometimes a lonely process. But the act of sharing your work should not be. Sharing should be a process that involves others: one that is social, and one that feels as natural as a conversation with a close friend. When you talk to a friend, do you tell them again and again about something you created, and how amazing it is? Likely not. Instead, you tell them about your process, what motivated you, the roadblocks, and so much else about what drives you. In communicating your journey, you open your friend up to the world of your creative work, and it encourages them to feel a part of your journey. The result is that they become advocates for what you do, and they forge new paths to help others reach your gateway. On these same paths, they will walk one of their other friends through the gate. And that friend will do the same with someone else.

I have heard many others say that the most powerful form of marketing is word-of-mouth marketing, meaning that the most powerful way to drive sales or awareness of something is by a friend telling a friend. I believe this to be true as well. Why? Because there is a high trust factor between friends, and the communication likely happens at exactly the right time that the person needs it.

Sharing the journey is about developing advocates around your creative work that lead to word-of-mouth marketing. It also feels amazing, because you develop connections with people who appreciate what you do and why you do it. Walking people through the gate is the practice of engaging others with your creative work.

Sharing is Engaging

In your field, I'll bet you have seen people who endlessly promote their work. Perhaps they are an author and they use Twitter to just constantly share the same series of Tweets promoting their novel. It is always a pitch with a link to Amazon, or the 20th reminder that their book is on sale, or they are trying out three new hashtags to try to find new readers. That person is using social media as one would use a press release — blanketing the town to see whose attention they catch.

If the most important part of your gateway is your creative work, I want you to consider the second most important part to be the people who share your enthusiasm for the same kind of work that you craft.

What that means is that these people who share your enthusiasm are more important than all the following things:

1. **You — your ego and identity.** I have seen many creative professionals who have such a desire for validation, a need for a sense of pride in what they have created, that they feel sharing online is their "one chance" to finally shine. So they act with less generosity. They focus too much on promoting their own work (again and again), not just because of ego, but out of a feeling that they have invested years of effort to have reached this point. They are convinced that this is their one moment to not blow it. Are "ego," "pride," or "external validation" bad things? No! They are fine. All I'm asking is that you balance them with sharing a sense of enthusiasm that engages your ideal audience.

2. **Clever marketing ideas.** With so many blogs and podcasts sharing tips on how to market your work, I have found that many creative professionals are drowning in an unending to-do list of "clever marketing ideas." They try one. When it fails, they try the next. Then the next. They find it difficult to really invest in one specific strategy because a new one is always dangling in front of them like candy. They always feel behind because it seems that everyone else has it figured out, except for them. They can't focus on the audience they already have, or find practical ways to grow it slowly, because there is always another click-bait headline that seems to deliver "the answer" to growing their audience or selling more of their work. When it doesn't, they are confronted with yet another click-bait headline.

3. **Things you paid for that represent your work.** I can't tell you how many creative professionals I have met who spent months of time and lots of money having a static "thing" created, and now feel they need to

justify the expense by constantly promoting it. This could be a website, book trailer, poster, brochure, logo, business card, or something similar. There are two sides of this coin. First, way too much time is wasted in creating these things. Why do people insist on making them? Because it makes them *feel* professional. Let's say an artist hires a web designer to create a "home for their artwork on the web." Quickly, this comes to represent everything about how they feel about their work, and how this website represents who they truly are. They spend months getting this designed, and because they paid a lot of money for it, they have high expectations for how it should work on their behalf to drive engagement with an audience. It usually doesn't work, because it's not one of the two most important things in the creative process. It's not the creative work itself and it's not the experience that work creates for an ideal audience.

4. **The image you have painstakingly crafted.** In an effort to feel a sense of validation, many creative professionals craft a "brand" surrounding their creative work. It can include some of the things above, but can include so much else, including how they describe their work — the descriptions, biographies, descriptions, taglines, etc. — that elevate the importance they feel it deserves. Then, they hide behind this. Just like the wizard in the movie *The Wizard of Oz*, they fear they are not as big or impressive in real life as their image portrays. The image becomes a projection meant to portray strength and professionalism. The problem I find is that it creates a distance between the creator and those they hope to engage. The artist can no longer share with their ideal audience because

they are too busy trying to seem distant and professional. They write their biography in the third person because it sounds bigger; they only share positive news, not proper status updates that share the reality of how complex their lives are; they don't show enthusiasm for other people's work because they feel it diminishes their own importance; they can't show their actual process, because they fear doing so will show the "little man behind the curtain."

5. **Your social media numbers, or numbers at all.** Before mobile phones, many people used to have a Rolodex on their desk at work or home. It contained individual cards, on which were written the name and phone number of each person they knew, all bound together. In an office, this would not only be a useful tool, but a signal as to how important you were. The bigger the Rolodex, the more people you knew, and therefore the more powerful you were. Today, nothing has changed. When we view social media, there is a key distraction that can become overwhelming: seeing how many people follow someone on social media, such as Twitter, Facebook, Instagram, YouTube, and the like. If these numbers were private, not public, it is likely that a person would be thrilled to have 350 followers for themselves and their art on Instagram. The problem is that the numbers are public, which means we see others who have 3,500 followers or 350,000 followers. Suddenly, they feel insignificant, and their followers seem insignificant compared to this. They begin focusing on gaining more followers instead of really engaging those they already have.

With your creative work, what matters is the work itself,

how you have grown as a person as you develop your craft, and how your work affects the lives of others. To walk people through your gate, consider how you can give people a *way in* to it.

The Four S Process

The way to venture out in the world is a system I call the Four S Process. If your work is meant to give people hope, for example, you can:

1. **Seek** out others. Identify places where people tend to look for signs of hope, and where they hang out online and off.
2. **Signal** to others that you are like them, and are welcoming a chance to engage. This indication can be your demeanor, a sense of shared interests, facial expressions, or how you speak.
3. **Share** things that represent hope. Perhaps you talk about who inspires you and why.
4. **Shape** conversations by asking questions. Take a small action to help or engage. People walk around all day surrounded by pushy messages and unscrupulous, untrustworthy salespeople who want to take from them — take their time, their attention, and their resources. Be the one who gives instead of takes, who asks about them first instead of rushing to tell them about yourself.

Seale's Four S Process

I want to share an example of what applying the Four S Process looks like in real life. I am going to use an example of someone who is *not* focused on their creative work. I do this because I find that some of the most compelling ideas for you to better grow your audience are found by looking outside the borders of your topic, genre, or field. When seeking examples to help guide you, the question you want to ask yourself is, "Who is doing work that matters and is succeeding at it?"

Since I work with a lot of writers, I tend to befriend people who work in publishing. One of those people is Seale Ballenger. He works in high-level publicity roles, and has worked directly with many bestselling authors, including Rick Riordan, Mo Willems, Alexandra Bracken, Bill O'Reilly, Lauren Bacall, Joe Hill, Neil Gaiman, and John Grogan. Beyond his regular duties at an office, he accompanies authors on book tours, which involves an incredible amount of planning, travel, and bouncing from one event to another. In other words, he is incredibly busy. He has to juggle a lot of balls and answer to a lot of different people.

However, on Facebook, I often see Seale share updates about the cities he is visiting, the places within that city where he has gone, and he typically shares a story about someone he has encountered who looks down and out. Often the people are homeless or people going through extraordinarily difficult situations. He approaches them, buys them a meal, chats with them for a while, and then shares their story with his Facebook friends. Sometimes he seeks these people out, noticing the one person on a crowded train platform who needs help. But as I scrolled through the many stories he shared on Facebook, I noticed how often it was someone else who initiated the interaction with Seale. They said they were hungry, asking if he could buy them a cup of coffee or spare some change.

I have ignored literally hundreds (if not thousands) of these requests in the many years I have spent in New York City. To be honest, these types of requests can feel like the background of life in a city, akin to the sounds of car horns, brakes screeching, or the muffled voices of a distant conversation. I do not say that out of pride; I share it to illustrate how easy it is to dismiss these signals. If you came to me and asked the simple question, "Dan, if someone came to you in need, would you help them or ignore them?" it would be easy for me to answer, "Without question, I would help them." Yet in hundreds of cases on the streets of NYC, my actions have been otherwise; I have ignored requests for help. How do I justify this behavior? Sometimes it can be via skepticism over whether they are truly in need or if they are conning me. But most times, I justify it as "I'm too busy."

But not Seale. He has honed his ability to notice and respond to others in need. In other words, the signals are all around us, but we don't always pick up on them. Seale does. Here is how Seale moves through the process of the Four S Process:

- **Seek.** As described above, he seeks out others and is receptive to those who ask for help. When I walk down the street, I am either focused on reaching my destination or lost in my own thoughts. But Seale has a sense of radar which allows him to be aware of those around him and pause when he sees someone needs help.
- **Signal**. Seale greets these people with a smile and openness. In a city environment, a signal as simple as a smile, or even eye contact, can be rare as thousands of people brush past each other on their way to somewhere else, with their own concerns.
- **Share.** In the situations Seale is in, buying coffee or a meal is often the trigger that frames the experience. He is not promoting anything about himself; he is handing someone sustenance as a way of communicating who he is and what he cares about. This is an

act of generosity.

- **Shape.** Seale shapes where this goes by initiating a conversation. He asks questions, and, perhaps most importantly, he listens. These are people who are ignored by thousands of others on the street every day — people like me — and here is Seale, listening intently to them. What he is doing here is not focusing on a transaction, saying, "I bought someone coffee." Instead, he is a gateway for them to experience kindness. Then, Seale extends this further by sharing that person's story on Facebook.

Now, this isn't a book about creating more empathy in the world or being a do-gooder; I understand that. You are a creative professional who wants to develop an audience around your work. Let's translate Seale's story with your goals.

Seek Out Others

Embrace others who craft similar work as you, or share enthusiasm for it. Don't think of others in your field as competitors. Instead, think of them as collaborators. It can be tempting to feel competitive with others, because they may have what you want, and you may feel that there is only a limited amount of success to go around. It's easy to think that the way to succeed is to steal the success that someone else is experiencing. "After all," you may say to yourself, "there are only so many fans of the kind of work I create," or "There is a limited amount of money spent on this type of work per year; I want to increase my piece of the pie."

That kind of thinking will greatly limit you, because you are only able to envision having what others in your field have created for themselves. Instead, embrace the idea that the more your colleagues succeed, the greater the chances you have to succeed. Instead of feeling envy or jealousy of others, I would encourage you to overwhelm them with kindness. Interview them, promote their work, and befriend them, because they are not what will hold you back. Too often, what holds a creative professional back is their own inability to forge the relationships they need within the field in which they work. These people know your ideal audience, and that audience knows them. Invest in those relationships.

Likewise, seek out those who share an enthusiasm for this type of work. For example:

- If you are an author, seek out other authors who write in the same topic or genre as you do. Show up to their events, email them, support their work. Be curious about their readers. Ask them questions about what they love and why.
- If you are a crafter, attend craft fairs not just to check out the products for sale, but to make a point to talk to the sellers, those who organize the event, and especially the customers who are browsing.
- If you are a musician, go to shows and talk to roadies, stage managers, people working the events, and of course, the fans.

In other words, the people you hope to engage with are all around you. Don't wait for them to find you—be perceptive and seek them out.

Signal to Others That You Are Like Them

Consider the emotions your ideal audience wants to experience. Appealing to people's emotions is a very effective way to grab their attention and hold it. This process begins with empathy. Focus on a range of emotions someone can feel around your creative work, and not just, "Look how amazing my thing is! Now buy it!" Very often a work of art is created because of a deep drive within the creator. We can't always see that on the surface—but we want to. The emotions that drive you, the experience others have with your work, and the change you hope your work makes in the world are the signals that you put out in the world.

There is a simple practice that too many creative people miss: share the emotion you want others to feel when they experience your work. This practice focuses on experiences, not "things." Someone is no longer buying a rectangle with paint on it—they are buying an experience that is priceless. The emotion they feel is a big part of this. These emotions could evoke:

- Joy
- Confusion
- Inspiration
- Loss
- Curiosity
- Caring
- Struggle
- Hope
- Victory
- Rejection

Note that these do not need to be positive emotions. They

can be challenging, provocative or even pensive emotions, as certain modern art evokes. They can be emotions that marry deep honesty with big proclamations, like certain slam poetry evokes. Consider the emotions 1980s heavy metal music sought to evoke. Musicians felt anger and rage at those who looked down on them, or held them back, and wanted their listeners to feel it to, too. In other words, the emotions your work evokes do not always need to be "joy," or "inspiration," or "thoughtfulness."

Emotions of any kind act as a signal and give people a way in. When an artist says, "I want my paintings to give someone a sense of hope," it's easy to see the emotion of "hope" as a direct way for them to engage their ideal audience. When "hope" is what aligns their audience to their work, it's clear what kinds of people they should seek and what sorts of messages they should use to engage them. We can imagine this artist venturing out into the world to connect with actual individuals, not sitting behind a table at a craft fair simply waiting for their ideal audience to walk by and notice them.

Share Your Enthusiasm and Creative Process

Our culture has become obsessed with how things work. Just look at the rise in cooking shows that take us behind the scenes in kitchens all over the world. Or how "professional" grade cooking supplies are now available at your local Walmart, indicating that we are no longer satisfied in our own kitchens to have tools that are merely "good enough"; when we cook, we want it to be exactly like the professionals.

Deconstruct why the type of work you create is special and take people behind the scenes to show how it is done. Doing so helps them appreciate the craft and provides you another way to engage people.

This also allows people to feel that they are a part of the

process of creating something. If someone attends a twenty-minute presentation on glass blowing, they feel that they are part of the craft because they now understand the steps. In your creative work, share the process, the materials, the milestones, and educate them on the elements of what makes incredible work.

Likewise, you can share what drives you on a deeper level. If you are a painter, you don't have to only show when you put paint to canvas—you can share how you find inspiration. Perhaps you find inspiration by taking long walks in the woods—share that. Or perhaps you do a lot of research in libraries, seeking out rare and old books—share that.

These are motivations and processes that people can relate to and find a connection to.

Shape Conversations by Asking Questions

I find that those who are successful tend to be curious. They ask questions that others overlook, and by doing so, they discover meaning where others do not. Be curious about those you meet as you work through the Four S Process. The most effective way for you to engage with others is to have a keen sense of empathy, to learn about what drives them, and to craft conversations that connect this to your own drive and creative work.

Find Models Outside of Your Own Field

It is helpful to find models for success that embody the Four S Process. I suggest you look for people whose work you admire who also share behind-the-scenes examples of how they have grown their career. It's not that you want to copy them, but rather that they can help inspire and illustrate the practical ways that success happens. The trick, though, is to look outside of your own field.

When you only look within your field, you find that people tend to emulate the same strategies and tactics. When you look outside of your field, you find new ideas that would feel refreshing to your ideal audience. I find YouTube to be a wonderful way to find and learn from models for success. Here are two examples of people who have inspired me recently:

- Casey Neistat is a gateway for filmmakers. He shares his work, his process, and behind-the- scenes stories on his YouTube channel. He ran a 600-video experiment where he shared a video of his life every single day. You see how he organizes his studio, how he collaborates with others, and how he crafts his philosophy for working. This led to a growth in his subscriber count from 500,000 to more than six million.

- Adam Savage is a gateway for makers — those who want to design, develop, and build things. Most know him from the TV show "MythBusters," but I only discovered him via his YouTube channel. He takes you inside his workshop, shows you in detail how he designs and builds things, and profiles others who do the same. He demystifies and deconstructs complex projects, breaking them down into steps I can understand. But more than that, he shares his enthusiasm in a way that is infectious. In doing so, he has made a wide range of skills feel more accessible to me. Adam no longer has his own TV show, but he still engages his audience of two million fans each week via YouTube.

What I have found is that Casey and Adam are also

gateways for those outside of their field. Their millions of followers are not all filmmakers and makers, and you will often see comments from their audience that Casey was the reason someone began making videos, or Adam was the catalyst for their first big project.

If you are a musician, a painter, or a writer, there is so much you can learn from Casey and Adam about what it means to share your work and engage an audience. If you check them out, one thing you will notice is their incredible generosity. How they make time for individual fans, support others in their field, and have a wide network of professional relationships. That is the next step you must take—to ensure your gateway connects with people by focusing on individuals, not "an audience."

Focus on Individuals, Not an "Audience"

We dream of having "an audience." But in doing so, we can diminish the experience of the individual who appreciates our work. We overlook them because we are so focused on building a crowd around our work. Crowds are made of people, and they often begin with one or two advocates drawing others over to see what is so special about what you have created.

Instead of "audience building," focus on one person at a time. Too often, people look at those who are successful, noting how generous they are in signing autographs and in engaging in conversation. If you stand outside of a venue where a band performed, hoping to meet the musicians, you can hear people walk away afterwards saying things such as, "The singer didn't sign anything; he was such a jerk," or "Wow, the drummer talked to me for five minutes. What an amazing guy!"

Engagement at this level can shape how people feel about you, and can trigger whether they decide to share your work with their friends. In other words, generosity is a core part of word-of-mouth marketing.

Taylor Swift famously engages with fans on a one-to-one level. She will show up at a fan's wedding and sing; she will pick out personalized Christmas gifts for specific fans and hand-deliver them. Does it sound like a marketing shtick? Go on Google and look up "Taylor Swift Blank Space Wedding" or "Taylor Swift Gift Giving 2014." Now, I have never knowingly listened to a Taylor Swift song, and while I respect her and her music, I'm not a "fan" in any sense of the word. But watching these videos showcases the power of the experiences that an artist can create for others. It is emotional and creates moments that people can't help but talk about and share. Here I am, a non-fan of Taylor Swift telling you about how amazing she is, and how you should go look up these videos. That is what she has created by being engaged and generous.

Many of my readers will view the Taylor Swift videos and be inspired, yet ignore these practices in their own work. Why? Because when you have sixty email newsletter subscribers for your artwork, it can feel like small potatoes. You likely know most of those sixty people and are seeking greater outside validation. You say, "Sure, when I am as big as Taylor Swift, I can make time for my fans on a personal level." Why would you say that? Because it inherently feels validating when you have millions of fans, and once you are validated, you think that *then* you will have the wherewithal to give back and be generous?

I challenge that kind of thinking. I contend that you need to develop those practices now. You need to look at those sixty people and not wish it was 160 or 1,600, but appreciate them and their connection to your work.

Often, I hear people bemoan how things were better in "the good old days" when we didn't have social media and when there wasn't so much distraction. They felt that before the Internet, they could more easily get their book read, have their music heard, or build an audience for their art.

I disagree. I think it was painfully difficult to find an audience before the Internet.

The Beatles were a group for six years, and played more

than 200 shows before they got a record deal to record their first album. Three record labels rejected them before this happened.

Even decades later, success wasn't any easier for bands. I remember hearing an interview with Blur bassist Alex James who was reflecting on their success in the 1990s. He was surprised at how much work it took to get known, and then once they were famous, how much work it took just to stay on top. There were constant interviews, radio spots, gigs, and appearances. They had to struggle in the beginning, and he felt that it never got much easier. It was always way more effort than he would have expected for the simplest step forward.

This was my experience as well. Let me share a few stories that illustrate how pathetically I failed at finding an audience for my creative work in the 1990s.

You know those people I just mentioned who complain, "I only have sixty followers on Twitter!" Well, in the 1990s, I *dreamed* of having sixty followers.

Sixty people to show up to an event.
Sixty people who cared about my art.
Sixty people who would share my music.

In the 1990s, I ran a music fanzine, had a band, did a lot of art, and managed a bookstore cafe that hosted live performances. Sixty people could have made a difference to each of those experiences, and in my life as a whole. Yet it was painfully difficult to even reach that milestone, and in most cases, I failed.

My 1990s Music Zine

A zine (or fanzine) is a mostly handmade magazine

created by a fan. In the 1990s, I had a music zine that focused on Britpop and space rock. A friend and I published around a dozen issues, filled with original interviews and reviews. We published it ourselves, spending late nights at Kinko's, and paid for hefty printing fees at a time when I earned minimum wage.

It's not like the endeavor paid off, either. We had a single advertiser, and publishing this zine left me thousands of dollars in debt when I was still in college.

By any measure today, this zine would be an unbelievable failure. The audience was mostly the reviewers we roped in to write for us and the guy behind the counter at the record shop as we tried to convince him to leave a stack by the door.

The funny thing about all of this? The record labels loved us. They sent us loads of free CDs and tapes, gave us free concert tickets, and I was able to interview all of my favorite bands. I was able to chat with musicians from Blur, Oasis, They Might Be Giants, and many other bands, all at the height of their success.

But, with all of this work, we couldn't even gather a tiny fan base for our zine. Did people pick it up and flip through it at the record store before throwing it in the trash? Maybe. But we struggled to develop any kind of meaningful connection even to a single reader.

It's worth noting the reason the record labels gave two guys from New Jersey so much access to the bands, because that's part of the pre-Internet story, too. It was impossibly difficult for the record labels to promote these bands. The time we took putting together a zine was enough indication that they should treat us really well, even though we had pretty much no audience whatsoever.

The better the record labels treated us, the more I realized how desperate they were to find any kind of promotion and outreach effort that was effective.

My 1990s Art

When I was a kid, I was the "artist" in my family and in school. My brother always had me draw the covers to his book reports, and I was allowed into special art programs at school.

In the 1990s, my life was filled with art project after art project. I did illustrations, paintings, pop-up books, sculpture, photography, and so much else. I would travel to out-of-the-way stores in New York City and New Jersey, spending hundreds of dollars on art supplies. I accrued (even more) credit card debt that took years to slowly pay off.

Whenever friends or new people I met talked to me, I likely told them about one of these projects. I remember having a grand plan to do oversize sculptures akin to those by Claes Oldenburg, one of my favorite artists. He's the guy who constructed large-scale sculptures of everyday objects; for example, a three-story tall pair of binoculars which served as the entrance to a building on Los Angeles

My dreams were always bigger than my reality. I made art late into the night, while juggling three part-time jobs, most paying minimum wage, or close to it. To get my work in front of an audience required skills I didn't seem to have, and resources of energy and money that eluded me.

Sure, I would visit The Center for Book Arts in Manhattan or the Printed Matter bookstore, but I was mostly a tourist. By this, I mean that I rarely engaged with others there, and never became a true part of the arts communities surrounding these places. I spent weeks preparing a book that was submitted to Printed Matter, only to have it rejected. I moved on to another project after that, then another, then another.

This felt frustrating. Each new art project brought a renewed sense of hope, but over the years, without anything fanning the flames, the fire in my art went out. I moved on to other projects.

The Attic

Where does most of this art and music now reside? In cardboard boxes in my attic. Remember that final scene of *Raiders of the Lost Ark*? The one where someone puts the Ark in a crate, and then puts it in a warehouse filled with thousands of identical crates? That sums up the way my creative work from the 1990s reached an audience. In other words, it was hidden from view.

Back then, it would have been amazing to open a shop on Etsy for my art, or to post images of my works in progress on Instagram. Having had sixty people validate this work would have made a huge difference in my quest to stop dabbling and really try to share my work in a bigger way. Having a single person who encouraged me would have meant the world to me. Sixty would have made me double down on my art, instead of letting it languish.

In these years, I tried many other creative projects as well. I had a band, I became a photographer, and I wrote poetry. All if it is mixed in those same cardboard boxes up in the attic. Of course, these acts lead to me honing my skills, and meeting an amazing array of collaborators. These early failures made me appreciate the value of what it means to connect with a single person who appreciates your creative work, hence this very book that you are reading.

But still, I would have loved to have had sixty followers for this work. To look out onto an audience of sixty people who cared. To have had sixty people waiting for my next painting. Today, that is much easier, when you consider that I could:

- Release songs on SoundCloud to reach sixty fans.
- Create a blog or podcast instead of a printed zine, not only saving me thousands of dollars in printing

costs, but increasingly the likelihood of reaching the first sixty fans that my 1990s zine never did.

- Post my artwork (or prints of it) for sale on Etsy, not only establishing a fan base, but earning a revenue stream in the process. To be paid for your creative work is a powerful milestone.
- Share my photography on Instagram, and connect to those first sixty fans by using hashtags, as well as connecting with other photographers whose work aligns with mine.

For each of these, I could also establish a two-way communication with these fans via social media, email, video, and so many other ways.

My experience in the 1990s wasn't just observing how my own creative work failed to reach an audience. I saw this constantly as the manager of a local bookstore cafe that hosted performances. Week after week, I watched people share their poems, their art, and their music. Sure, some nights were grand, with people flowing through the door. But many were a mixed bag, including nights of nothing but crickets as a response to someone's song. Polite applause came from the barista. You would witness people's hopes and dreams die right there and then: it was heartbreaking. To have had an email list of sixty subscribers or be able to connect with our customers on Facebook would have been wildly more effective than what we were capable of at the time.

My point is, if you have sixty followers, treat them like the most special people in the world. They are the foundation for how your work will reach more people, and impact the world.

Create Experiences, not Data

Many creative professionals are frustrated with social media because they hoped it would be a shortcut to success, and instead it is simply another communication channel by which to engage with other human beings. How do we solve this? By aligning with this quote:

"Frustration stems from focusing on what we don't have. The antidote is appreciating what's already here." — Leo Babauta[14]

Build your audience one person at a time. Do so by connecting with others long before you feel you are ready to "launch" your work. Many creative professionals don't share with the world before they share their work, because they are worried it isn't ready yet. They believe that the air of mystery will somehow elevate their launch to making a "splash." Instead of waiting, bring people along for the journey. Not only will it help you establish and grow an audience now, it will become the engine for word-of-mouth marketing down the road.

Here are some practical ideas to get started valuing the audience you have, no matter how small:

- Connect with one new person per week. Take them out to lunch, email them, or set up a phone call.
- If you have an audience of any sort, focus on engaging more with the top ten percent, those who seem to be more supportive. Put more effort here than you do into worrying about attracting new people.
- Send an email to a colleague — a mid-level doer who practices the same craft you do — and thank them for how their work inspired you.
- Interview those who do what you would love to do. You can ask them everything you ever worried about in your own work, but also share the interview to promote them and become aligned with them publicly.

When you focus on the depth of connection first, you craft experiences, relationships, and memories that lead to a sense of fulfillment around your creative work. This is priceless when compared to trying to "game the system," seeking out artificial ways to boost social media metrics.

If you are like many people I speak with, you may feel a sense of frustration that you can never reach the tipping point with connecting your work with more people. The truth is, you need assistance. It's time to develop a support system for your work.

Develop a Support System

People dread admitting to others that they need help. It feels safer to project the illusion that you are not vulnerable. I encourage you to seek out others who can assist you and create processes for them to do so. In other words, create a support system to join you on your journey.

First identify collaborators, those who will help you in your process of bringing your work to the world. If you look back to some of the processes we have already been through — bringing people to your gate, befriending guides, the Four S Process — you will find that you already have identified people you have connected with and can potentially take the next step with in order to create a support system for your work.

Too often, writers, artists, musicians, and others who do creative work have a romantic notion of "going it alone." Their vision feels so personal that they can't imagine a process whereby they allow others in. They dream of crafting their work alone in its "purest" form, then sharing it with the world and having people magically discover it and be moved by it.

But the truth is your work will spread because of those with whom you share your journey. Relationships are a major part of success, not because of corruption, such as someone bypassing an otherwise fair system by pushing a friend's work ahead in the line, but rather because relationships are about trust and understanding. When you surround yourself with people who understand your work and trust you as a person, you are creating powerful forces to ensure your creative vision spreads.

Collaborators also address the challenge of sustainability. Too many people with creative visions let it die at the first failure. Surrounding yourself with those who can support your work and support you as a person when you are unsure of the path forward can be a critical stepping stone from uncertainty to success. These people act as your support. Sometimes that is in directly supporting your work, but other times, it is supporting your own uncertainty and doubt.

What is the biggest thing that will keep your work from being created, discovered, and appreciated? You. You are the most dangerous force that will stop your work from reaching others. You will stop too soon. You will get distracted. You will try, and fail, and then give up. You will be convinced that a different idea is better; then another; then another; constantly hopping from one idea to the next. You will tell yourself that success wasn't meant for you; you will become bitter that others had a leg up.

Build the support system you need to ensure your creative work reaches others by embracing collaborators. Consider how each person you connect with becomes a collaborator — someone who is part of your creative process. Types of collaborators to consider:

- Those who connect with your ideal audience every day.
- Those who share similar goals to yours.
- Those who share different, but complementary goals.
- Those who can help you be social.
- Those who help you do the work you don't want to do (create graphics, schedule updates, edit blog posts).

- Those who help you establish a more effective creative process.
- Those who help you communicate more effectively. I had a client whose husband was able to better communicate what her book was about than she was. I would ask her a question about her book; she would ask her husband, and he would concisely answer in a single elegant sentence. The books she wrote were 100% hers, hundreds of thousands of words, but the ability to sum it up in a sentence was done better by someone with a tiny bit of distance — her husband. He was a wonderful collaborator.
- Those who can help you brainstorm marketing ideas.
- Those who can help you balance your time and energy.
- Those who can help you manage the financial aspects of your creative work. Money is an incredibly emotional thing to manage; sometimes we need the advice of others to know where and when to invest in our creative work, and how to balance the fear that most people have around financial decisions.

Finding collaborators is key to making creative work sustainable. I have been an artist or writer for nearly my entire life and have countless friends in the arts. Again and again, I have seen projects that were full of life suddenly deflate because the artist was crushed under the weight of all of they were trying to manage by themselves. They had zero support. Rarely did their work die because an external force killed it. Instead, it was killed by the creator who couldn't work out their own process for sharing their work with the world. The result was that they simply couldn't persist and their creative work languished.

For collaborators, start small but intentional. You don't

even need to hire these collaborators as you begin. Many of the most powerful collaborators you have are not those you will pay. You simply need someone who can be a sounding board when you have questions, and keep you on track and accountable. The key to this is not having the expectation that the collaborator can magically fix everything. If you want someone to help answer questions, you have to be clear and concise in what you ask, and you have to actually be willing to act on that person's advice. If you want someone to keep you accountable, you have to illustrate to them that you will do the work, even in the moments they aren't prodding you. In other words, don't punish the person for being a collaborator by having unrealistic expectations of their role.

Let's look at some practical examples of how to integrate collaborators into your life, so they can help you walk your ideal audience through your gateway.

1. Find Mentors

These can be formal or informal relationships. You could approach people who you respect or are successful in your field and ask to shadow them, apprentice with them, or meet once per month for them to share advice. Or you could consider informal mentorships. Identifying people in your life who you can check in with on a regular basis, but without them having to agree to officially be a mentor for you. For instance, there may be a craftsperson who runs a shop in town, where you can stop in twice per month to view their work and maybe ask a question. You may have people you interviewed (if you conducted some of the steps from previous chapters) who might be willing to let you ask some follow-up questions about your own work. Send them an update email once per month, where you tell them how you are acting on their advice and thank them for their help. For every second email, ask a simple question that you could use their input on.

I can already sense the fear that this suggestion raises in people. "What if I'm bugging them? What if I'm being too needy? What if I'm interrupting something important?" Think of it this way: Wouldn't it feel nice to receive an email from someone who indicates that you are wise; that you have helped shape their life in a profound way; and that your advice is, every day, improving them further? These are the kinds of notes people dream about receiving: not someone just sucking more of their resources, but indicating that their work has had an impact on the world. The key difference is the tone of your communication. If you reach out to someone who is prominent in your field and ask them to spend an hour having lunch with you so you can "pick their brain," then I would agree that this is a lopsided value proposition for that person. They are likely surrounded with people who want their time and attention. But what if you are the person who asks nothing, but gives quite a bit? What if the small things you do ask for are framed in a way that illustrates the impact that they will make?

Perhaps this kind of outreach puts a bad taste in your mouth for another reason, though. Perhaps you don't want to put someone in the role of being a mentor because it means you are subservient—LESS THAN—to them. Many creative professionals I speak with have decades of experience behind them, and feel that now is their time to finally receive recognition. The very idea of reaching out to interview someone, ask a favor of someone, and seek a mentor feels like an affront to everything they have worked for.

Let me give you an example of how powerful this effect can be. Podcasts have seen a renaissance in the past few years, and one popular form is the interview podcast. Here, the podcaster brings guests on the show and spends the entire episode asking them questions. This has been a key way for someone who has no standing with a community to gain recognition and connections, by aligning with those more prominent than they are, and because of the relationships that are formed in the process, they develop a powerful network of people in the field.

This is what Andrew Warner did in interviewing more than 1,000 entrepreneurs for his podcast, *Mixergy*. One by one, he went from a guy who was simply asking questions to someone who others seek out for speaking engagements and mentoring. Srini Rao did something similar with his podcast, *Unmistakable Creative*. After years of asking questions on his podcast, he landed a two-book deal with a major publisher on what he learned in the process. Why did he get a book deal? Likely it was a few reasons, all which indicate the value of this methodology.

1. He developed his public voice and following, one episode at a time.
2. He learned and learned and learned by asking questions.
3. He developed a powerful network of colleagues.

Consider what a publisher wants from an author, and how these three things are a perfect match: someone with a strong voice and following, who has wisdom to share, and comes to them with a powerful network of prominent people who may help market the book for them.

This process can work even for people who don't need to start at square one. As an example, we can look to Tim Ferriss, who was already a bestselling author, sought-after speaker, and angel investor by the time he began his podcast, *The Tim Ferriss Show*. What did he do? The exact same things that Srini did above. The effect is even more powerful because Tim was starting from a place of greater prominence. He was able to secure interviews with those who were much more famous than him; people that other podcasters would never be able to gain access to.

He extended his voice in the public not by being louder, but by going deeper. His interviews ranged from one to three hours, and he went deep. Like Srini, he turned this experience into his next book, *Tools of Titans*, in which he shared the wisdom he learned by gaining access to these people. What's more, he explained how the advice he has received from these people has been integrated into his own life—further showcasing the value of their work.

I am not asking you to create a podcast. I am simply using these stories to illustrate the value of reaching out and developing relationships with those who can mentor you, and in doing so, help you more effectively lead people to your gateway. It's a shift to viewing the concept of "collaboration" in ways other than signing with a publisher, record label, gallery, agent, or the like. All of this is to make the point that people you can learn from are much more accessible to you than at any other point in human history. Sure, you can try to make an excuse—"Dan, these people don't want to receive another email asking something of them," but that is just an excuse. Learn from Andrew, Srini, and Tim. The opportunity is there, if you are willing to take it.

2. Establish a Mastermind Group

One of the most powerful things I have ever done to move my career forward, and feel more fulfilled within it, was establishing a mastermind group. This is not a networking group, whereby the goal is simply a way to get more business by providing business to others in the group. Rather, it is a group of people who help encourage and support each other's goals and daily creative practices. I have been a member of quite a few mastermind groups, and I will take you through three ways they can be structured.

- Small group mastermind. The first mastermind I was a part of was with three other people, each of whom worked in different creative fields than I do. Twice a month, we would meet via video chat online, as we all lived in different parts of the country. The rules were simple. Each person was allocated one-fourth of the call (20-30 minutes) to tell the group about a specific challenge they had or a goal they were working toward. The rest of their time was spent brainstorming ideas and ways of helping them navigate.
- One-on-one mastermind. The small group can be re-mixed as needed. I am part of another mastermind that involved only one other person; we speak weekly via the phone, and devote one call to her challenges and one to mine.
- Managed mastermind group. This is where one person acts as the leader of the group and actively manages the group by giving prompts, sharing ideas, and encouraging collaboration. I have run many of these, usually with ten people per mastermind. There are similarities to the small group mastermind in that the members come from different creative fields, have different goals, and are asked to hone in on specific challenges and goals they need assistance with. I typically run these groups entirely online using a group chat program and videos. The members have the ability to chat and post updates 24/7; because of this, I was amazed at how many friendships formed within the group, and how as a whole, it became a tight support group.

There are many other ways to engage in mastermind groups. They can have more structure and a greater commitment to take specific types of actions each week. They can be more actively managed or more fluid. The three examples above have had a profound effect on me and my work, and in helping me learn to walk people through my gateway. I am not left guessing who my audience is, what resonates or how to reach them. By engaging with mastermind groups, I have established a daily process to find out in simple, practical ways.

There are many other ways to identify collaborators, including hiring help, such as consultants, coaches, part-time staff, or interns. I won't dig into those, however, because I understand that as you craft your gateway, you may not have financial resources to invest. The ideas above are powerful ways of identifying collaborators without any financial costs.

How can collaborators, mentors, and masterminds help you walk people through your gate? Three ways:

1. By helping you better understand those you want to reach and how to effectively communicate and engage with those people.
2. By telling you practical stories of what did and didn't work for them.
3. By allowing you to gain perspective from another person of how they interpret the messages and work you are crafting.

This is the critical step in the process. This book alone isn't all you need to craft your gateway. I don't know you, your creative work, the niche you work within, or the people you hope to engage. Find people that do, and identify ways to collaborate with them. Learn from them, and vet your ideas through them. Become a student of this process, and ensure that you are doing field research.

I describe this process as you are walking people through your gate because you need to establish a sense of empathy for what that experience is like, which will result in you making many small adjustments to ensure it truly engages others. Creative work fails to find an audience when the creator assumes a specific intrinsic value within it that their ideal audience is never able to see or experience because the creator didn't make it clear to them.

Walking someone through the gate is a process of helping others experience your work, by having empathy with how they see the world.

Perhaps you are nervous that walking people through your gateway requires a lot of social interaction, and you are thinking, "That has never been my strong suit. Maybe there is another way, one where I don't have to engage with others." That is fear talking—the biggest barrier standing between where you are and what you dream of achieving. In this next chapter, we'll dig into how to move past this fear.

Fear is Your Biggest Barrier

Too often, we think our biggest barrier to success is lack of resources or money. Or that we don't have the right connections. Or we don't have enough knowledge. Or we don't understand the trends. Or our timing is bad. But the real barrier is fear. We resist stepping out of our comfort zones to connect with others who can help us share our creative work and develop our audience.

Actor, producer and screenwriter Charlie Day framed it this way in an address he gave to the 2014 graduating class of Merrimack College:

> *"You cannot let a fear of failure, or a fear of comparison, or a fear of judgment stop you from doing what's going to make you great. You cannot succeed without the risk of failure. You cannot have a voice without the risk of criticism.*
>
> *People will tell you to do what makes you happy, but a lot of this has been hard work, and I'm not always happy. I think you should do what makes you great. Do what is uncomfortable, and scary, and hard, but pays off in the long run. You don't have to be fearless, just don't let it stop you."*[15]

The idea of forging relationships with collaborators can be off-putting for many creative professionals for three reasons:

1. Hiding your creative ideas, because you feel this is the foundation of your identity.
2. Fear of losing control of your creative work.
3. Social fear.

Let's explore each.

Barrier #1: Hiding Your Creative Ideas

Many creative professionals do their work amidst many other responsibilities in life. Oftentimes, their creative work can be the only thing that provides them an identity they are truly proud of, that feels like their own true expression of who they are and what they are capable of. The idea of involving others who are collaborators threatens that identity, because suddenly they fear that by sharing it, others will corrupt it. They love the validation that comes from their work and the image that it is a true expression of who they are. The moment that they involve others, they fear the work may no longer be their own. They want this to elevate their sense of personal identity, not lessen it.

When will these people welcome collaborators? When the stature of those collaborators raises their own identity. For instance, a writer may eschew any collaboration whatsoever because they want their novel to be a pure expression from their heart, but they will welcome signing with a prominent publisher because doing so validates their writing and identity as a writer. In other words, there is a transactional nature of embracing this type of collaboration. Simply saying, "My book is being published by XYX publisher," is akin to saying, "My work matters; I can finally call myself a `writer' and not feel self-conscious."

But when we seek this type of validation—from a publisher, gallery, record label, or others—there is a cost. You are welcoming dozens of collaborators into your process, few of whom you will ever meet. They will shape your work, and in many cases, they will outright own your work. While I love publishers, galleries, and record labels, I simply want you to understand the transaction you are making in seeking out collaborators.

Author John Green gives a wonderful summary of the value his publisher and collaborators bring to his work:

> *"I wouldn't have any books to my name without the tireless and committed collaboration, not only of my editor, my agent, my friends, my family, everyone at [my publisher], but also the thousands of other people — copy editors, warehouse employees, programmers, people who know how to make servers work, librarians, and booksellers. We must strike down the insidious lie that a book is the creation of an individual soul, laboring in isolation."[16]*

This is why I am encouraging you to embrace collaborators early in your process so you can learn what truly engages an audience. The day you sign with an agent, a publisher, or a label is not the culmination of your work, but a core part of how you communicate your work to others.

Barrier #2: Fear of Losing Control of Your Creative Work

Often people don't share their creative ideas and processes with others because they fear someone will steal them, or they will lose control over them. Why? Because often, our creative work feels like a "way out," or a lottery ticket we have purchased. It represents our own personal path to our dreams. But don't confuse your idea with the execution of the idea. One thousand people could "steal" your idea and do it in one thousand different ways, but none of them will pursue your idea with the same vigor and creative energy that you will. You can't reduce Harry Potter down to "wizard school," and think someone can steal the idea and create something as great as Harry Potter.

When you covet your idea, you put limits on it. Instead of seeking out all the people who can help you, you spend your time closing every door you can.

Barrier #3: Social Fear

If you are like most people, the thought that this process requires social outreach will make you nervous. This is not my goal; in fact, I think there is a way to do this that lessens your social fear, while also increasingly the chances for success in leading people through your gateway. Let me give you an example. When I was in my twenties, I really enjoyed throwing parties. I'm one of those people who had a lot of social anxiety about attending parties because I could never figure out how to socialize in a natural way. I didn't like walking into rooms where I didn't know anyone, didn't know how to start casual conversations, and would basically cling to one person the entire time as a way of dealing with my anxiety.

I found, however, that when I hosted a party, there were ways I could navigate around all of my anxieties which allowed me to be very social in ways that made me comfortable. For instance, everyone at the party would be someone I knew, or someone who was a guest in my home. I had a relation to everyone because of this. Because I was the host, I had a job to do, which kept me busy; I couldn't experience social anxiety when I was busy. I could easily talk to anyone at the party because I could ask if they needed anything and introduce people to each other. I never had that moment of loneliness of being a wallflower, because I stayed busy ensuring the party was running smoothly. It turned out my challenge wasn't that I couldn't engage with people; it was that I needed a safe context to do so, and one that had a structure to it. What's more, I actually *enjoyed* being social in this other context.

The irony is that an outsider would look at me, hosting parties with dozens of people attending, and assume I am an extrovert. Yet I'm not. The parties were my way of being social and managing my social anxiety and introversion. To help people walk through your gateway, experiment with ways to make the social aspects of this fun and reduce the amount of anxiety you may feel.

The stories you tell, the experiences you craft, the moments you share — this is your gateway. Not the number of Twitter followers you have. To see your gateway in action, walk people through it, one by one. In practical terms, this is all about developing simple practices of reaching out and having simple conversations using what you have.

Walk Someone Through the Gate

Walking someone through your gate is a process of finding out who that person is, what drives them, and how your gateway aligns with their own path. Don't assume that once you have crafted your beautiful gateway and the realm that lies beyond it, people can actually reach it. This is where creative professionals go wrong. They assume too much:

1. That the signs leading to their gateway are clear and engaging.
2. That the travelers are looking for what they offer beyond their gateway.
3. That the paths to it are not blocked.
4. That there is nothing along these paths that would make people apprehensive.
5. That these people have everything they need to take this journey on their own.

To find out is a process of challenging your assumptions, but this is not some academic exercise. Instead, you are going to have to walk people again and again down the path that leads to your gateway. By doing this, you will learn new things about what motivates those you hope to engage, and you will learn where your "strategy" for engaging others with your work was, in fact, you being willfully ignorant of the gap between your intention and the needs or desires of those you hope to engage. Let's go through some practical ways that you can find out by walking people through your gateway.

Finding Out #1: Experiment Strategically

As a creative professional who hopes to engage a wider audience, you are likely always hunting for aspects of your work that capture the interest of others. Sometimes it is in the way you describe your work; other times you may adjust the work itself based on feedback from your audience. For instance, if you are a musician describing your work, you may find that when you say, "My music is alt-folk," people don't express much interest. But when you say, "My music is like Leonard Cohen meets Kraftwerk," people nearly always show enthusiasm.

Likewise, if you are a performing artist, you may notice that people respond to the single a cappella song you sing in the middle of your show. Because of this, you may expand that to a mini-set of three songs, or you may even consider recording a track this way for a future album. In both of these examples, you are observing what resonates, and changing your behavior to encourage others to engage with your work as well.

This very book is an example of walking people through the gate to find out what resonates. When I first used the term "gateway," it was not with the intention of writing a book. As part of the small mastermind group I run, I record and share a video every day. These are impromptu videos to share advice. Several months ago, without any forethought, I recorded a video where I riffed on this idea of the gateway. There were around ten people in the group, and this video really resonated. They kept referencing it in the online chat in the days afterwards. I took notice and decided to see if this "gateway" concept had legs outside of the mastermind. Perhaps it was a fluke, and this small group only liked it because of how intimate our relationship was. So a couple weeks later, I decided to write a blog post on the topic and then sent it to my email list. Again, I received a big response via email.

I proceeded to explore why people liked this concept, and began mentioning it in interviews and online chats I was a part of. Then, I began hearing people say the term "gateway" back to me. They would write about it in their own blogs or just use it in an offhand way as they described their process. I found that the concept of the gateway attracted people to my work, and helped them make sense of their own. So I doubled down on it by writing this book. That involved taking a 1,500-word blog post and turning it into tens of thousands of words.

I didn't just come up with an idea that I thought was clever and decide that it should be a book. I kept engaging and sharing with my ideal audience, and listened to what resonated. When I found something, I kept exploring it and growing it. It was a process of finding out, not assuming. I did so across multiple channels: my private mastermind, video, blog, email newsletter, webinar, interviews, private emails, and private phone calls. Why? Because all of these channels connected me with other people, which is what matters more than the channel itself. Too often, a creative professional will ask what social media channel they should focus on. My answer is simply the one that allows you to connect meaningfully with real people. And in truth, that means you should use a wide range of communication channels and methods, not just one social network.

Let's consider how you can connect with your audience across different channels with a different example. You may be an author who schedules a book reading at a local bookstore. Too many authors will book these, but then they just wait for people to find their event. This is akin to building your gateway in the woods and waiting for others to find it. They don't want to do the work required of clearing the path, posting guideposts, and befriending travelers. Instead, they want others to do that work. They sit back and hope that the world simply makes it easy for them, so they don't take action.

I was speaking to a children's author I know who does take action to drive people to her events and author visits. For a school visit, she described some of the steps she took:

- Creating and distributing flyers ahead of time to parents, so they can order the books.
- Donating a portion of the profit from each book sold to the local library.
- Giving away copies to the teachers for their classrooms.
- Taking out ads in the local newspaper.
- Creating, printing, and hanging posters in local stores.
- Buying something fun to give to the kids, which she works into her presentation.

I know this sounds like a lot of work, and it is. Why would she do this? Because she is doubling down on the opportunities she does have instead of doing nothing and "waiting to see" if anything magically happens at her events without her making much effort. Do you need to do all of this? Absolutely not. But I would encourage you to view opportunities to engage others with your work as experiences you craft, and as a way for you to learn more about who you are hoping to capture and what drives them.

Identify ways to experiment to find out what works. Put yourself in the position to have to ask your ideal audience what drives them, or find ways to observe them in action. For instance, if you are a folk musician, go to other people's shows. Then, instead of sitting in the corner trying to look cool, talk to people. Ask them how they heard of the band, where they traveled from to get here, who else they listen to, and how they heard of the show. Observe if they came alone or in a group, what their age is, and if they dance or just sit and drink.

You don't have to do this in person. You can reach out to fans of other creative professionals online via email or social media. You can observe how audiences engage with the artists on social media. This isn't just for musicians. If you are an author wondering if book readings are an opportunity for you, consider doing the following:

- Watch five videos per day of author events on YouTube. There are untold thousands of these. Notice what the author does and what the audience does. What works and what doesn't.
- Email five authors who recently went on book tours and ask them three short questions via email.
- Call ten bookstores. Ask them about how their author events work and what makes a great one. If they don't do author events, ask them why and what drove this decision.
- Identify three authors who are currently on tour, and observe their social media during that time. Look for their own updates on Twitter and anyone who mentions their name. Look for videos uploaded to YouTube or photos shared to Instagram.

Then, experiment for your own work. You don't have to convince a bookstore to give you a reading in order to do this; perhaps your first book isn't even published yet. Instead, hold a literary salon in your living room, at the local library, or as part of a local organization. Don't worry about promoting your own work. Instead, experiment with what creates an event that attracts and engages people interested in books similar to yours. You can go back through the many examples in this book to help it get off the ground, such as identify collaborators and co-hosts.

If you dream of speaking to audiences, don't wait until you are "big enough" to hold your first event. Do it now. Do it consistently. Learn more about what works and what engages your ideal audience by conducting many experiments.

Finding Out #2: Start Small, and Grow as You Learn

Perhaps the examples above still seem like too much. I say that with complete empathy; perhaps you are a single mother of three who works full time, and in the few spare moments you have, you are writing a memoir. You are reading this saying, "But Dan, I have no time and no resources. How can I begin from where I am?"

Start with *one thing*. Focus on one question you are asking, and take a single action each week. This can be a simple prompt, such as, "How can I ensure my memoir truly helps young women who were in the same situation I was in twenty years ago?" That can begin with taking a single action around research from earlier in this book—identifying comparable authors, asking advice, identifying collaborators, etc. But it can extend beyond that, like identifying how your story can change the life of a single person. Because if you can do that, you can change the world with your creative work.

Look around your community. Where would you be able to find a young woman in the situation you were in twenty years ago? Are there organizations that do outreach? Are there specific neighborhoods where you could talk to local faith-based organizations? Or specific schools? Put yourself in the position to show up and observe. Begin asking questions. As a single mother of three who works full-time, that won't be easy. Perhaps there is a volunteer event you can attend as a family. Or perhaps you can make some phone calls during your lunch break. Maybe you can stop by different places on your way home from work.

The goal is not to launch a campaign, but to identify one person you can help. Your ultimate goal may be, "Sell a million copies of my memoir, and ensure each one helps give a young woman the self-esteem she needs to change her life for the better." But for now, focus on this: "Can I speak to one person who I can give a sense of hope?"

Learn from this experience, then iterate. Perhaps it leads to you writing an article for the newsletter of one of these local organizations, or running a Saturday workshop for three of its members. Or interviewing local people for the newspaper, where you highlight specific needs.

When you walk a single person through your gateway, you learn so much about their needs, desires, and preferences, and how they relate to your creative work. Perhaps you learn fifty percent of what you need to know to forge new paths to your gateway. Then, walk a second person through, again doing so with empathy and care. Really pay attention to them. Double down on these people—don't look past the individual because you are so focused on engaging "an audience." Invest in the people who are right in front of you and who are interested in your work.

As you walk people one at a time through your gateway, you are more firmly establishing the path to it.

Finding Out #3: Create Experiences, Not Content

Your goal in this process is not to build some big "launch," but rather, to change one person's life with your creative work right now by crafting meaningful experiences. Too many creative professionals are blinded by this idea of a big launch, where one day they wake up and go from having no audience to going viral. This often revolves around them focusing on content alone. While writing an article, creating a podcast, or creating a social media strategy may feel like "audience engagement," it isn't. Sure, they can be a part of the process, but too many people use them as stand-ins for actual engagement.

Instead, focus on creating experiences. Creating a blog post that you hope leads to someone reading it and maybe even clicking the "like" button for it isn't true audience engagement. Seek out conversations and connections with individuals — something that is specific and truly social.

It takes *effort* to create experiences. Too often, we hide behind the safety of content. For instance, if you were holding an event around your creative work — a book reading, a gallery show, a product launch, or a performance — you may consider having cupcakes made that feature your artwork as the icing. It's clever, and it feels like branding, but at the end of the day it's just content, because it doesn't create a unique experience any more than a bag of Doritos in a bowl would. Someone sees the art, maybe smiles, eats their cupcake, and the moment is over.

What if you did what Chris Sacca, an early investor in companies such as Twitter, Uber, Instagram, did instead? Here is the advice he gave on Tim Ferriss' podcast for creating a fun party:

> *"If you can bring one thing to make an amazing party night, it is wigs. Mullet wigs change everything." He brings a bag of*

166

seventy-five mullet wigs to parties and just lays them out somewhere on the side of the room. He doesn't announce it or force people to wear them. Instead, he lets people find them on their own. He found that this kicks the party up a notch and allows each person to pick a wig that they feel represents their own personal style. In many ways, it helps people shed their usual inhibitions, and creates a new experience with themselves and those around them.[17]

It can feel like a risk to bring wigs to a party, or to have them at your own. There is the outlay of money, the fact that no one asked for this. One could worry, "What do wigs have to do with my work?" Again, this is where you need to focus more on the experience you create for others and less on simply providing content.

What experiences can you create around your gateway?

Musician and author Amanda Palmer calls this "seeing you." She does this by holding a gaze that is longer than one normally would with someone who she feels needs help. She describes it as,

"My eyes would say – 'Thank you. I see you.'
And their eyes would say – 'Nobody ever sees
me. Thank you.'"

Eye contact alone creates a memorable experience.[18]

Every day you have this opportunity. Instead of re-sharing the same links as everyone else on social media, instead of sending the same boring "professional" emails, why not be ludicrously kind and generous to those who support your creative work or creative work like yours?

If you are worried that this sounds crazy, put a safe boundary on it. Tell yourself that you will send one generous email per week for a month, a season, or a year. This can help you justify it in your mind, but also explain it to others — i.e., "One of my resolutions this year is to be kinder to people, so I'm sending one email a week to someone who inspires me."

Consider how you can give back to specific people in a huge way. Not Tweet about their book, but do something bigger. Create an experience and do it *really* well. Crazy well. The return on investment should be lopsidedly bad. Invest way more than you think you should. This can be as simple as taking someone out to lunch. Pay for the lunch, spend the lunch thanking them, and be interested in listening and helping.

If this sounds like too much giving, and not much receiving, then let me share one of my favorite quotes which I heard in a video Apple created in the early 2000s, profiling designers: "Caring is a powerful business advantage." This is from Scott Johnson, and it indicates how success happens, not by tricking people into discovering and buying your work, but by creating experiences that people remember and doing so on a human level.

Living on Both Sides of the Gateway

You are a gateway. The creative work you share, the way people discover it, and the interactions with you become the threshold someone moves through in order to be opened up to new experiences, new ways of seeing, and new possibilities. Consider the paths and conversations that lead people to your gateway, and the experiences you share once they move through it.

I encourage you to understand this as a human process, to have empathy for those you hope to engage, and in doing so, not just sell them more work, but truly create advocates in the process. When you connect the drive you have for what you create and the drive that motivates your ideal audience, you can help them walk through your gate and open up the possibilities you have created in your work.

Take Action

Now it is your turn to take action. For more resources on how to *Be the Gateway*, please check out this page of my website: http://wegrowmedia.com/gateway/ for resources and advice that expand upon this book, and share practical ways for you to take action. You can also sign up for my weekly email newsletter where I explore the concepts of *Be the Gateway* each week: http://wegrowmedia.com/newsletter/

You can connect with me on social media in the following places:

Twitter: http://twitter.com/DanBlank
Facebook: http://facebook.com/WeGrowMedia
Instagram: http://instagram.com/DanBlank
Thank you.

Endnotes

1. http://tim.blog/2015/09/22/scott-adams-the-man-behind-dilbert/

2. https://www.youtube.com/watch?v=DXwVD2ncqfE

3. http://www.gq.com/story/unexpected-john-malkovich

4. https://en.wikipedia.org/wiki/The_Only_Living_Boy_in_New_York

5. https://www.youtube.com/watch?v=AdKUJxjn-R8

6. http://www.thecreativepenn.com/2016/08/20/usa-today-bestseller-ad-stacking/

7. https://en.wikipedia.org/wiki/The_Great_Gatsby

8. http://www.dailymail.co.uk/news/article-2706801/The-Fault-In-Our-Stars-tale-doomed-teenage-love-entranced-millions-Now-author-reveals-inspiration-chance-meeting-bravest-girl-all.html

9. https://en.wikipedia.org/wiki/Brandon_Stanton

10. https://www.statista.com/topics/2501/etsy

11. https://www.quora.com/How-many-books-does-Amazon-have-for-sale

12. http://www.filmindependent.org/blog/dos-donts-submitting-sundance/

13. https://news.spotify.com/us/2013/10/07/the-spotify-story-so-far/

14. https://twitter.com/zen_habits/sttus/752157894322245632

15. https://www.youtube.com/watch?v=IulvPqb1Eus

16. https://www.youtube.com/watch?v=Pd4EFEfu0ww

17. http://fourhourworkweek.com/2016/01/15/chris-sacca-on-shark-tank-building-your-business-and-startup-mistakes/

18. https://www.ted.com/talks/amanda_palmer_the_art_of_asking/transcript?language=en

Acknowledgments

I would like to thank the following people who made this book possible:

My wife Sarah and my son Owen for the daily support that makes everything I do possible. Also our baby, who we are expecting as I write these words, for focusing my intentions.

My parents Michael and Barbara, and my brother Andrew, for their unwavering support.

Book coach Jennie Nash for the incredible guidance and her ability to challenge me to do better.

My team at WeGrowMedia for their daily execution filled with enthusiasm.

Diane Krause for her wisdom and advice on navigating the practical side of doing creative work.

The launch team for this book, and the members of my mastermind group whose daily collaboration has ensured I am always mindful of the reality of the daily lives of creative professionals.

And thank you, Starbucks. Not just for the coffee that fueled the creation of this book, but for the thousands of hours of free rent, free air conditioning and heat, and free electricity. Oh, and for the pleasant company of your baristas!

About the Author

Dan Blank is the founder of WeGrowMedia, where he helps writers and creative professionals share their stories and grow their audience.

He has worked with hundreds of individuals and amazing organizations who support creative people, such as *Penguin Random House, Hachette Book Group, Sesame Workshop, Workman Publishing, J. Walter Thompson, Abrams Books, Writers House, Kenyon Review, Writer's Digest, Library Journal*, and many others.

Dan's work has been featured by *Poets & Writers* magazine, the National Endowment for the Arts, *Professional Artist* magazine, *Compose Journal*, and 99u. You can find him at:

WeGrowMedia.com
Twitter at http://twitter.com/DanBlank
Facebook at http://facebook.com/wegrowmedia
Instagram at http://instagram.com/DanBlank

Made in United States
Orlando, FL
21 January 2022

13850080R00098